D0084550

The Urban Revolution

The Urban Revolution

Henri Lefebvre

Translated by Robert Bononno

Foreword by Neil Smith

University of Minnesota Press
Minneapolis • London

The University of Minnesota Press gratefully acknowledges financial assistance provided for the translation of this book by the French Ministry of Culture.

Copyright 2003 by Robert Bononno
Foreword copyright 2003 by the Regents of the University of Minnesota

Originally published in French under the title *La Révolution urbaine,* copyright 1970 Editions Gallimard.

All rights reserved. No part of this publication may be reproduced, stored in a retrieval system, or transmitted, in any form or by any means, electronic, mechanical, photocopying, recording, or other-wise, without the prior written permission of the publisher.

Published by the University of Minnesota Press
111 Third Avenue South, Suite 290
Minneapolis, MN 55401-2520
http://www.upress.umn.edu

Library of Congress Cataloging-in-Publication Data

Lefebvre, Henri, 1901–1991
[Révolution urbaine. English]
The urban revolution / Henri Lefebvre ; translated by Robert Bononno ; foreword by Neil Smith.
p.   cm.
Translation of: La Révolution urbaine.
ISBN 0-8166-4159-5 (HC : alk. paper) — ISBN 0-8166-4160-9 (PB : alk. paper)
1. Cities and towns.   I. Title.
HT151 .L375 2003
307.76—dc21

2002015036

Printed in the United States of America on acid-free paper

The University of Minnesota is an equal-opportunity educator and employer.

12 11 10 09 08 07 06 05 04 03   10 9 8 7 6 5 4 3 2 1

Contents

Foreword

Neil Smith

This translation into English of Henri Lefebvre's classic if contested text is long overdue. *La Révolution urbaine* first appeared in 1970, in the aftermath of the May 1968 uprising in Paris. Cities around the world from Detroit to Tokyo, Prague to Mexico City, were the scene of major revolts, connected less through any organizational affiliation than through political empathy linking highly diverse struggles, and as the 1960s culminated in worldwide challenges to capitalism, war, racism, patriarchy, imperialism, and the alienation of modern urban life, the book was inevitably received as a political testament to the possibilities for fundamental political and social change. Although the "revolution" of 1968, as it has come to be seen, ultimately failed, the appeal to urban revolution captured the aspirations of the period, and nowhere more than in Paris; it was as realistic as it was anticipatory, and the book became a pivotal if controversial intellectual text on the European and Latin American left. Along with some of Lefebvre's earlier work, it put the urban on the agenda as an explicit locus and target of political organizing.

Most surprising, perhaps, is that despite the turbulent

circumstances of its writing and publication, and especially despite Lefebvre's direct involvement in the events of the time, *La Révolution urbaine* is remarkably sober, politically if not always philosophically, avoiding both the wild effervescence of "the moment," as Lefebvre would have put it, and the suicidal agony of defeat. It expresses an inveterate hopefulness and openness toward the future that has often been hard to sustain in the three decades since its publication but which characterizes Lefebvre's philosophically induced intellectual and political optimism. At the same time, as an examination of this careful translation attests, this is no mere historical document. In some ways even more than when it was first published, it bears a strong sense of political immediacy and contemporary relevance. Lefebvre was seeing things at the end of the 1960s that many of us, often with his help, came to see clearly only in more recent years and now are still discovering. It is worth highlighting some of these issues by way of providing a few signposts to the text.

But first some biographical context. Born at the turn of the twentieth century in a small Pyrenean village in southern France, Henri Lefebvre came to political consciousness amid the horrors of World War I and the promises of the Russian Revolution. In the early 1920s he moved to Paris to study at the Sorbonne and became engulfed in an extraordinary creative, political, cultural, and intellectual ferment that mixed avant-garde artists with communists and a new breed of young radical philosophers. The eclectic range of influences on Lefebvre's political and intellectual development derived first and foremost from this period as he devoured Hegel, Marx, and Nietzsche, among others, as well as the emerging work of Heidegger. He joined the Communist Party in 1928, combining political activism with intense writing that, across the span of his ninety years, would eventually yield an astonishing string of book-length philosophical, political, and sociological studies. An emerging intellectual figure by the eve of World War II, he was forced from Paris and from his university post following the Nazi invasion and he lived out the war as a Resistance fighter in southern France.

Despite becoming one of its most heralded intellectuals, Lefebvre's relationship with the Communist Party was testy at best, and, as the party's Stalinism retrenched with the cold war closing in, he chafed more and more at the lines it took. As with so many others, his end came after the 1956 Khrushchev report unveiled the authoritarian violence and corruption of Stalin's regime; after an unsuccessful attempt to reform a recalcitrant party he was expelled in 1958. Over the next few years he published two books on Marx and two selections of Marx's work, but he also turned his attention to a series of questions that interested him deeply but on which the Communist Party leadership had often frowned. Via the themes of ideology, alienation, and everyday life, he returned to a long-standing concern with rural sociology and also picked up an earlier, broader, critical analysis of the quotidian in an effort to explore the political fabric and fabrication of the everyday. Although the rural focus continued, by the mid-1960s he turned his attention to the urban everyday, announced by *Le Droit à la ville* (The right to the city), still untranslated in its entirety into English. Between 1966 and 1974 he produced, in addition to several other titles, no fewer than eight books devoted to understanding the urban and, more broadly, the production of space (as he put it). "From Heraclitus to Hegel to Marx," Lefebvre once observed, "dialectical thinking has been bound up with time," and although his effort was most focused in this period, a central theme of Lefebvre's lifework involved the attempt to rethink the dialectic in terms of space. If, as Foucault once commented, the nineteenth-century obsession with history brought a "menacing glaciation of the world," Lefebvre sought to reinvigorate our grasp of modern capitalism by squeezing it through the neglected sieve of space. Along with

La Production de l'espace (1974; English translation, 1991), *The Urban Revolution* stands as the most enduring exploration from this period. It was and remains *the* pathbreaking analytical work connecting urban research not just with marxist theory but with social theory and philosophy, broadly conceived.

To appreciate the novelty of what Lefebvre was trying to do it is important to recall that urban research in the 1960s was dramatically undertheorized. Throughout the social sciences and especially in sociology, urban analysis was largely descriptive. Where it aspired to theory, most notably in the work of the Chicago school, which remained influential into the 1960s, or in the case of social ecology, urban research relied more on empirical generalizations than on theory per se. Innovations in social theory that helped codify the social sciences after World War I (the work of Max Weber, Freud, Malinowski, the Frankfurt school) largely avoided an explicit concern with the urban, even if the earlier theoretical work of Durkheim and certainly Simmel did help to frame a generally untheoretical urban sociology. Louis Wirth, for example, writing about "urbanism as a way of life," applied Durkheim's social positivism to advance the themes of the Chicago school. Questions of housing, industrial organization, segregation, or community development certainly arose in the social sciences but were generally framed in technocratic fashion according to the impress of liberal policy requirements. Marxist theory, constrained by no such injunction, provided little alternative: many marxists rejected the notion that the urban represented a specific social realm, and the postwar Stalinism of the communist parties was openly hostile to the proposal of an identifiable urban regime, arguing instead that the urban represented a superstructural appurtenance rooted in the basal social and economic forces and relations of production. This was Lefebvre's primary target. By focusing on what he identified as the urban revolution, he sought to turn this state of affairs on its head. As late as the 1960s it was a novel proposition that the urban had to be theorized: "The expression 'urban society,'" he says, "meets a theoretical need." At the same time he insisted that when it came to processes of urbanization, it made little sense to separate the experiences of capitalism and "socialism," as found "on the ground." In this sense, more than a decade after he disavowed party membership, *The Urban Revolution* represents a forceful rebuttal of the closed-mindedness of the cold war French communist party.

By "urban revolution," Lefebvre sought to connote a far more profound change in social organization than that symbolized by the momentary urban revolts of the 1960s, much as these were symptomatic of this larger picture. "Urban revolution" identifies a long historical shift, from an agricultural to an industrial to an urban world, according to Lefebvre's account, but it also captures a shift in the internal territorial form of the city, from the originary political city through the mercantile, then industrial, city to the present "critical phase," the harbinger of a certain globalization of the urban. Integral with these shifts, the image of the city also transforms, as do the concept of the urban and the ideology of urbanism. Long before the notion of "postindustrial society" became popularized in the 1970s, Lefebvre is rightly critical of the intent of such a label, yet at the same time his central argument is that the problematic of industrialization, which has dominated capitalist societies for more than two centuries, is increasingly superseded by the urban: "the urban problematic becomes predominant." The political crisis of 1968, he suggests, was more profoundly a crisis of urban society than a crisis of capitalist industrialism.

For English-language readers, one of the remarkable aspects of this book is Lefebvre's engagements with a broad range of social theorists whose work during the 1960s subsequently became influential in Anglo-American circles. Not all of these encounters are obvious or well referenced, but all are implicitly if not explicitly critical. Somewhat elliptically, Lefebvre appropriates Althusser's notion of "continents" of knowledge but immediately launches into a critical discussion of ideological "blind fields," before then using this topographic metaphor to frame the temporal transition from agrarian to industrial to urban worlds. His discussion of heterotopy clearly engages Foucault. Where Foucault's heterotopias are evoked almost randomly in relation to time and space—cemeteries, malls, rugs, brothels, colonies, gardens—Lefebvre envisaged heterotopias in a more critical register, rooting them in a sense of political and historical deviance from social norms. The archetypal heterotopias for Lefebvre are the places of renegade commercial exchange, politically and geographically independent from the early political city: caravansaries, fairgrounds, suburbs. Less successfully, in an oblique effort to distinguish scales of sociospatial reality, Lefebvre differentiates between the "global," "mixed," and "private" levels, and draws on the work of Pierre Bourdieu (but with Heidegger clearly hovering over the text) to designate the private as the "level of habiting." In the process he insists on a distinction between the place and process of habiting: "habiting" takes precedence over habitat or habitus. His discussion of the "blind field" of ideology, together with references to revolution in the streets, continues a long-term dialogue with the Situationists, particularly engaging Guy Debord's *Society and the Spectacle*, published a year earlier. Blind fields for Lefebvre are places cum practices that obscure constitutive sociospatial relations.

Much as *The Urban Revolution* expresses the rich intellectual and political ferment of Paris in the period, it also represents the unfolding of Lefebvre's own thinking. Many of the formulations in this text can be seen as precursors to arguments that are more fully developed and explored in *The Production of Space*, published six years later, and more familiar to English-speaking audiences. The discussion of heterotopy fades but not that of utopia, while the concern with "habiting" broadens into a much denser exploration of spatial practice and form. The concern with urbanism as an ideological blind field is likewise broadened into an interrogation of spatial ideologies; urban practice becomes a subset of spatial practice. And there is a clear continuity between the evolution from a political to a commercial to an industrial urbanity on the one hand and on the other the historical transition posited in *The Production of Space,* from absolute space to historical, abstract, and ultimately differential space. The continuities between these texts are real, but so too are the discontinuities. A political immediacy in particular marks *The Urban Revolution* as a quite different text from the more abstract and more expansive work of a few years later.

Whereas space came alive in early-twentieth-century art, physics, and mathematics, in social theory and philosophy it was a quite different story. Space there was more often synonymous with rigidity, immobility, stasis; space itself had become a blind field. For Lefebvre, by contrast, space holds the promise of liberation: liberation from the tyranny of time apart from anything else, but also from social repression and exploitation, from self-imprisoning categories— liberation *into* desire. Space is radically open for Lefebvre; he refuses precisely the closure of space that so dominated western thinking and in some circles continues to do so. Only when we pause to reflect on the radical closure of space represented by contemporary financial capitalists' visions of globalization, or left-wing parodies of the same, does the genius of Lefebvre's spatial insistence become clear. When *The Urban Revolution* was originally written, the world was certainly more open to change, but it was far less open to seeing political change in spatial terms. The very shift in political thinking to embrace a spatialized view of the world, in significant part due to Lefebvre's work, makes it difficult today to see how genuinely iconoclastic this position was. *The Urban Revolution* is a paean to the space of the city and to the possibilities of revolutionary social change that comes from the streets.

But this radical openness comes with costs attached. Whereas Lefebvre is unrivaled in the analysis of the circulation of signs, capital, meanings, and ideas into and out of urban space and exploring the possibilities for political change that result, he is less adept at ferreting out how certain social meanings become fixed, however temporarily, in and as space and place. In the present text he makes a synchronic distinction between "global," "mixed," and "private" levels of society, which are roughly equated with the state, the urban, and "habiting," respectively. In contemporary parlance this represents a halting effort at what might now be called a "politics of scale," but Lefebvre's reluctance, in deference to the openness of space, to allow this production of "levels" to crystallize into anything approaching coherent spatial entities forecloses our understanding of the political processes by which social assumptions are written into the scaled cartography of everyday places. In *The Production of Space,* intent on a unified science of space, he tackled this issue again, but backed away from the discussion of levels. Instead he proposed, as part of a well-known conceptual triad, the notion of "representational spaces." Although "differential space" becomes Lefebvre's spatial code for socialism, the future, always coiled in the belly of the capitalist beast, his philosophical insistence on the openness of space allows little hint at all about how that differentiation of space is made and remade. Yet the architectonics of scale, as he might have put it, become the most vibrant technology of spatial differentiation: the spatial arbiters of what gets empowered and what gets contained.

Lefebvre's treatment of nature is nowhere near as central

to his argument, but it does work as a kind of counterpoint to his sense of space. In the context of the late 1960s, Lefebvre was well ahead of his time in his willingness not only to take environmental questions seriously but also to theorize nature while criticizing the emerging environmental movement. Quite unlike the radical openness that characterizes his treatment of space, the treatment of nature is less nuanced. For Lefebvre the transition from agriculture to industry brings a fetishism of nature at the same time that nature is subjected to unprecedented ravages. The transition to urbanization brings a further shrinkage of nature, while the signs of nature, by contrast, proliferate; the steady, violent death of nature is matched by an obsessive "ideological naturalization" of society and the parodic reproduction of nature as denatured "open spaces," parks, gardens, images of femininity. In clear contradistinction to his treatment of space, nature for Lefebvre seems radically closed as a venue for political change. Whether this closure of nature drew from his early and enduring experience with the southern French peasantry and the steady erosion of peasant life or whether it simply continued a prejudice of certain narrow readings of marxism is not clear, but this putative connection would seem to cry out for an engagement with some of the contemporaneous work of Raymond Williams. In any case, the making of nature, unlike space, represents a cause for lament, even as he criticizes various romanticisms of the environmental movement. Space in the end retains an optimistic Hegelian a priorism vis-à-vis nature. Philosophically, the (unfulfilled) promise of Einstein's relativity theory, namely a recombination of space and matter in favor of the philosophical primacy of the latter, remains unglimpsed.

But it would be a regrettable mistake if *The Urban Revolution* were to be read simply through the lenses of Lefebvre's later work, which adopts the rubric of space more explicitly. The book's initial reception predated that work. Indeed, it might be suggested that in the English-language world *The Urban Revolution* has suffered insofar as several widely read critiques quickly saw the light of day in the 1970s, more than a quarter century before the book was finally translated, and these have established a certain pattern of response. By the same token, the prominence of these critiques has also heightened the anticipation for this English translation. With greater or lesser amounts of respect, Lefebvre's provocative thesis that the "urban problematic" not only globalizes itself but also supplants industrialization as the motive force of historical change was quickly critiqued by two other of the most prominent urbanists of the twentieth century. A student of Lefebvre and a witness to the Paris spring of 1968, Manuel Castells responded immediately to *La Révolution urbaine,* and his critique was triple-barreled. In the first place he identified a certain romanticism in Lefebvre's sense that urban propinquity created a unique quotidian environment available for future reconstructions of sociability and desire. A philosophical utopianism, he suggested, undergirds the enterprise. Second, more generally and more decisively, Castells challenged the very presumption that "the urban" represented any kind of coherent scientific object available for study; the urban, for Castells, was at best an ideological construction, requiring desquamation rather than exaltation. Third, and most viscerally, Castells objected to the fact that Lefebvre's announcement of the urban revolution displaced marxist analyses of history, politics, and economics: implicitly reinstating the party line about base and superstructure (an argument often erroneously attributed to Marx), Castells complained that Lefebvre moves from a marxist analysis of the urban to an urbanist analysis of marxism (*La Question urbaine,* 1972; English translation, 1977).

The second critique came not from Paris but from Baltimore. Completing a book that affected English-language urban social science much as *La Révolution urbaine* did in

France and elsewhere, David Harvey, recognizing both the importance of Lefebvre's text and the critical convergence with his own work, engages Lefebvre in the conclusion to *Social Justice and the City* (1973). For Harvey, despite the broad commonality of effort with Lefebvre, it was simply unrealistic that the contradictions between urbanism and industrial capitalism are now resolved in favor of the urban. Where Castells deployed a structuralist critique fashioned over a blueprint of marxism, Harvey came at Lefebvre with a political economic critique of the sort that typified (not least because of Harvey's own efforts) Anglo-American marxism after the 1960s. Harvey was certainly sympathetic to Lefebvre's assault on party dogma, but for him industrial capitalism continues to create the conditions for urbanization, rather than the other way around, and the surplus value produced by capital accumulation, and especially its mode of circulation, is the raw material out of which urban change crystallizes. Urbanization here is the excrescence of the circulation of capital. The global spread of urbanism, he concedes, is real, but the circuit of industrial capitalism still predominates over that of property capital devoted to urbanization.

The present translation comes at a time when Lefebvre is gone and both Castells and Harvey have significantly developed their ideas, but these critiques remain relevant both vis-à-vis the text itself and as regards our understanding of twenty-first-century capitalism. Castells has long since moved on from the structuralism that drove his early critique, and Harvey has engaged critically and decisively with the critiques of structuralism that were hatching in Lefebvre's work, as well as with postmodernism, with which neither he nor Lefebvre had much sympathy.

Castells's accusation of utopianism is, as readers will find out, precisely aimed yet, especially in the present context, off target. One of the strengths of Lefebvre, especially when viewed with the benefit of three decades of hindsight and in the context of a would-be twenty-first-century American imperium, is his indefatigable optimism that a different world is possible. This book stands as a thoroughly contemporary antidote to the sense that "there is no alternative" to capitalism, a notion popularized in the grim 1980s by British prime minister Margaret Thatcher and globalized in brutal form in the early twenty-first-century "war on terrorism" that, outside the blind field, is in actuality an endgame to the globalization of ruling-class U.S. power. That Lefebvre's political optimism appears to spring directly from his philosophy and from his social theory rather than from a detached, facile political ebullience is even more remarkable. As for the question whether the urban constitutes a real object of social science inquiry, the conditions of this critique seem to have been set by a strange convergence between a positivist social science that insists on an "object" of analysis and a structuralist reformulation of official marxism that embraces much the same presumption. To that end, Castells's critique mobilizes Louis Althusser against Lefebvre, yet even by the time of the English translation of *The Urban Question* in 1977, Castells was coming to see the formalism of this critique as excessive. On the other hand, the language of base and superstructure, which also appears in Lefebvre's text, seems by the beginning of the twenty-first century to be thankfully obsolete.

The remaining critique, that industrial capitalism still provides the framework for urbanization rather than the reverse, as Lefebvre claims, needs to be taken more seriously. If in quite different tones, Castells and Harvey in the early 1970s effectively agreed in their critique: urbanization, powerful as it was, in no way supplanted industrialization as the motor of capital accumulation. This insistence might be written off as merely a defense of marxist political economy: certainly Lefebvre's argument would seem to challenge the

economics
& the
urban

theory of surplus value or at the very least to suggest that the historical development of capitalism increasingly circumscribes the validity of the theory in favor of something else. But that something else is never theorized. If Lefebvre is correct, it would presumably be important to know how the political economic transition from industrialization to urbanization operates. That is neither a rhetorical point nor is it a question that Lefebvre himself addresses in any systematic manner. His answer is oblique and incomplete. Thus by the time he wrote *The Production of Space* he had reconstructed the orthodox teleology of modes of production—primitive communism, slavery, feudalism, capitalism, socialism—into his evolution of space: absolute, historical, abstract, and differential spaces. Although it might seem like an obvious overture to argue that the supersession of industrialization by urbanization marks the transitional moment from abstract to differential space, in the language of the later work, Lefebvre resists this move. Instead, by the time he writes the four volume *De l'état* in the mid-1970s, he is barely concerned with urbanization and theorizes instead about (among other things) the globalization of the state. It is not at all clear how we are to fit together the victory of urbanization over industrialization, the production of space, and the globalization of the state.

Yet on several levels there is something empirically very appealing about Lefebvre's argument. First, purely in quantitative terms: As Lefebvre was writing *The Urban Revolution*, just over a third of the world's population was urbanized, according to United Nations statistics. By 2002 the figure was almost 50 percent. The most explosive growth has been in countries that in the 1960s would have been considered "Third World" but that have now undergone perhaps the most rapid industrialization and urbanization in history. Between 1970 and 2000 Mexico City grew from a population of 8.8 million to 18.1 million. Similarly, São Paulo went from

8.3 million to 18 million. Both have superseded New York City. Bombay (Mumbai) grew in the same period from 6.2 million to 16.1 million, and is projected to supersede the New York metropolitan area by 2005. Only Tokyo/Yokohama is larger than these three rapidly growing metropolises. The language of world cities and global cities emerged in the 1980s, but already in 1968, prior to most of this explosive urban growth, we find Lefebvre talking explicitly about "world cities" (in fact, he attributes the concept to Mao). But there is more than simply a quantitative aspect to the dominance of the urban, and here the relationship with industrialization is intense. The true global cities of the twenty-first century may well be those large metropolises that are simultaneously emerging as production motors not of national economies but of the global economy. Industrialization and urbanization are more, not less, interwoven, and the cities of most intense population growth are also those of greatest industrial expansion. In any case, as this language of world cities indicates, the transformation of urbanization is tied to transformations at the global scale captured, however ideologically, in the language of globalization: as Lefebvre sensed, the evident quantitative growth of urban areas does indeed express a much more complex shift.

Most urban growth has taken place at the periphery of the world's larger cities, whether as functionally integrated suburban development, industrial expansion, or burgeoning squatter settlements and favelas. But something symptomatic is happening in urban centers at the same time. Lefebvre remarks on the gentrification ("embourgeoisement") of urban centers, but that process, too, has changed dramatically since the 1960s. There are of course significant large-scale precursors, such as Hausmann in Paris in the nineteenth century, but the contemporary experience of gentrification dates to the post–World War II period and is usually associated with small-scale renovation of neighborhoods that had experienced major economic disinvestment. Since the 1980s, gentrification has become increasingly generalized as a strategy of global urban expansion. Central urban reconstruction increasingly integrates residential with all other kinds of land uses—offices, retail, recreation, transport—and is also increasingly integrated into not just the overall urban economy but into the global economy. A highly mobile global capital increasingly descends to and aspires to the remake of urban centers. At the same time there is a more seamless collaboration among property capital, the state, retail capital, and financial capital than at any previous time. This process has probably gone farthest in Europe, where neoliberal "urban regeneration" (a label Lefebvre would have abhorred as patently ideological) has become official urban policy in the European Union and in individual states as well as cities. The massive reconstruction along the Thames in London exemplifies the way in which gentrification generalized has become a highly significant part of the city's productive economy. Nor is this process restricted any longer to cities in Europe, North America, or Oceania. From Shanghai to Beirut, Kuala Lumpur to Bogotá, the reconstruction of urban centers has become the means of embedding the logics, threads, and assumptions of capital accumulation more deeply than ever in the urban landscape. One can see here a glimmering of the conceptual inversion Lefebvre poses between the industrial and the urban.

It is a deliberate part of Lefebvre's style to pose exaggerated opposites in order to force the dialectic forward. It is of course a style he shares with Hegel and Marx and many others. Different readers will surely interpret differently the argument that urbanization supplants industrialization and conclude differently about the veracity or usefulness of the argument. It may well be that in this stark form the argument is less useful than when seen as part of a larger tendency, a logical as much as historical movement with uncertain end.

Certainly this is how Lefebvre interpreted his own notion of "the complete urbanization of the world." The point was not that the planet was already fully urbanized and rurality forever gone but that the tendency toward that end was very powerful. The distinction between urbanization and industrialization may well be more important as a means to get us to recognize this point rather than as an enduring reality.

Finally, a word about Lefebvre's style. Evoking the diminutive name of the small genera of birds (titmice) and the exquisiteness of their gemlike eggs, the Scottish poet Hugh MacDiarmid once explained his own lifework: "My job, as I see it, has never been to lay a tit's egg, but to erupt like a volcano, emitting not only flame but a lot of rubbish." Without in any way indicting the quality of Lefebvre's work, I think, judging by the sixty-six books that pepper his life's work, that this French poet of social theory and philosophy must have approached his work in a similar fashion. At times, especially to English-speaking audiences, his writing can come across as a stream of philosophical consciousness that mixes coherent analytical agendas with fascinating diversions, apparently casual or completely intended, that might double back or end abruptly, before picking up the thread of the argument again—or stretching for a related thread that the reader must struggle to connect. Lefebvre is always suggestive, reaching, pushing his argument farther than he would later want to go in order to get a point out, less than direct, retracing steps, electing a different path. He always embraces a tension between rigor and fantasy, hard-nosed critique and political desire, which is why he is so exciting to read. He embodies the magic of a marxism liberated from dogma, yet this philosophical adventurousness also makes it fairly easy to find apparent paradoxes in his work. Recognizing that he rarely if ever provides a linear argument, these nonetheless have to be taken seriously, but there is a larger picture. Lefebvre actually gives us the braided complexity of the tit's nest, paradoxical interweaving and all, together with a clutch of delicate eggs laid along the way. This present text has its share of diversions but it is also well directed. His dearest desire in this book is that the eggs laid would hatch and that the "urban problematic" would give way again to a new generation of urban revolutionaries and urban revolutions. But why, Lefebvre wants to know, have the eggs of urban revolution not hatched before?

The aftermath of 1968 tested Lefebvre's optimism. As with so many others, not just in Paris but around the world, he had thought that revolutionary change was at hand, and, defeated as they were, they were only half wrong. In the conclusion to this text Lefebvre makes a wistful comparison between Paris in 1968 and the extraordinary political, cultural, and social transformations that took place in Russia in the 1920s while the revolutionary moment remained alive. Such leaps of optimism are precisely what makes this text not simply contemporary but forward-looking. The tremendous creativity of Russia in this period has had to be destroyed and forgotten by those enforcing the "blind field"—before 1989 but especially afterward—in order to justify the global consummation of capitalism. But the globalization of everything, as Lefebvre might have put it, cannot possibly succeed. An antiglobalization movement that wants to build a new anticapitalist internationalism can take a lot of inspiration from the ferment in Russia in its pre-Stalinist days, but it can also learn a lot from Lefebvre's insistence on urban revolution and the prospect of a globalized creativity, urban and otherwise, delinked from the effects of a ubiquitous economic and ideological slavery that Lefebvre understood as so deadening, but which he knew could never win.

1 || From the City to Urban Society

I'll begin with the following hypothesis: Society has been completely urbanized. This hypothesis implies a definition: An *urban society* is a society that results from a process of complete urbanization. This urbanization is virtual today, but will become real in the future.

The above definition resolves any ambiguity in the use of our terms. The words "urban society" are often used to refer to any city or urban agglomeration: the Greek polis, the oriental or medieval city, commercial and industrial cities, small cities, the megalopolis. As a result of the confusion, we have forgotten or overlooked the social relationships (primarily relationships of production) with which each urban type is associated. These so-called urban societies are often compared with one another, even though they have nothing in common. Such a move serves the underlying ideologies of *organicism* (every urban society, viewed on its own, is seen as an organic "whole"), *continuism* (there is a sense of historical continuity or permanence associated with urban society), and *evolutionism* (urban society is characterized by different periods, by the transformation of social relations that fade away or disappear).

Here, I use the term "urban society" to refer to the society that results from industrialization, which is a process of domination that absorbs agricultural production. This urban society cannot take shape conceptually until the end of a process during which the old urban forms, the end result of a series of *discontinuous* transformations, burst apart. An important aspect of the theoretical problem is the ability to situate the discontinuities and continuities with respect to one another. How could any absolute discontinuities exist without an underlying continuity, without support, without some inherent process? Conversely, how can we have continuity without crises, without the appearance of new elements or relationships?

The specialized sciences (sociology, political economy, history, human geography) have proposed a number of ways to characterize "our" society, its reality and deep-seated trends, its actuality and virtuality. Terms such as "industrial and postindustrial society," "the technological society," "the society of abundance," "the leisure society," "consumer society," and so on have been used. Each of these names contains an element of empirical or conceptual truth, as well as an element of exaggeration and extrapolation. Instead of the term "postindustrial society"—the society that is born of industrialization and succeeds it—I will use "urban society," a term that refers to tendencies, orientations, and virtualities, rather than any preordained reality. Such usage in no way precludes a critical examination of contemporary reality, such as the analysis of the "bureaucratic society of controlled consumption."

Science is certainly justified in formulating such theoretical hypotheses and using them as a point of departure. Not only is such a procedure current among the sciences, it is necessary. There can be no science without theoretical hypotheses. My hypothesis, which involves the so-called social sciences, is based on an epistemological and methodological approach. Knowledge is not necessarily a copy or reflection, a simulacrum or simulation of an object that is *already* real. Nor does it necessarily construct its object for the sake of a theory that predates knowledge, a theory of the object or its "models." In my approach, the object is included in the hypothesis; the hypothesis comprehends the object. Even though this "object" is located outside any (empirical) fact, it is not fictional. We can assume the existence of a *virtual object*, urban society; that is, a *possible object*, whose growth and development can be analyzed in relation to a process and a praxis (practical activity). Needless to say, such a hypothesis must be validated. There is, however, no shortage of arguments and proofs to sustain it, from the simplest to the most complex.

For example, agricultural production has lost all its autonomy in the major industrialized nations and as part of a global economy. It is no longer the principal sector of the economy, nor even a sector characterized by any distinctive features (aside from underdevelopment). Even though local and regional features from the time when agricultural production dominated haven't entirely disappeared, it has been changed into a form of industrial production, having become subordinate to its demands, subject to its constraints. Economic growth and industrialization have become self-legitimating, extending their effects to entire territories, regions, nations, and continents. As a result, the traditional unit typical of peasant life, namely the village, has been transformed. Absorbed or obliterated by larger units, it has become an integral part of industrial production and consumption. The concentration of the population goes hand in hand with that of the mode of production. The *urban fabric* grows, extends its borders, corrodes the residue of agrarian life. This expression, "urban fabric," does not narrowly define

urban fabric

the built world of cities but all manifestations of the dominance of the city over the country. In this sense, a vacation home, a highway, a supermarket in the countryside are all part of the urban fabric. Of varying density, thickness, and activity, the only regions untouched by it are those that are stagnant or dying, those that are given over to "nature." With the decline of the village life of days gone by, agricultural producers, "farmers," are confronted with the *agricultural town*. Promised by Khrushchev to the Soviet peasants, agricultural towns have appeared in various places around the world. In the United States, aside from certain parts of the South, peasants have virtually disappeared, and we find islands of farm poverty alongside islands of urban poverty. As this global process of industrialization and urbanization was taking place, the large cities exploded, giving rise to growths of dubious value: suburbs, residential conglomerations and industrial complexes, satellite cities that differed little from urbanized towns. Small and midsize cities became dependencies, partial colonies of the metropolis. In this way my hypothesis serves both as a point of arrival for existing knowledge and a point of departure for a new study and new projects: complete urbanization. The hypothesis is anticipatory. It prolongs the fundamental tendency of the present. Urban society is gestating in and through the "bureaucratic society of controlled consumption."

A negative argument, proof by the absurd: No other hypothesis will work, no other hypothesis can cover the entire range of problems. Postindustrial society? Then what happens after industrialization? Leisure society? This addresses only part of the question, since we limit our examination of trends and virtualities to "infrastructure," a realist attitude that in no way circumvents the demagoguery inherent in this definition. The indefinite growth of mass consumption? Here, we measure current indices and extrapolate from them, thereby running the risk of reducing reality and virtuality to only one of their aspects. And so on.

The expression "urban society" meets a theoretical need. It is more than simply a literary or pedagogical device, or even the expression of some form of acquired knowledge; it is an elaboration, a search, a conceptual formulation. A movement of thought toward a certain *concrete,* and perhaps toward *the* concrete, assumes shape and detail. This movement, if it proves to be true, will lead to a practice, *urban practice,* that is finally or newly comprehended. Needless to say, a threshold will have to be crossed before entering the concrete, that is, social practice as understood by theory. But there is no empirical recipe for fabricating this product, this urban reality. Isn't this what we so often expect from "urbanism" and what "urbanists" so often promise? Unlike a fact-filled empiricism with its risky extrapolations and fragments of indigestible knowledge, we can build a *theory* from a *theoretical hypothesis.* The development of such a theory is associated with a *methodology.* For example, research involving a virtual object, which attempts to define and realize that object as part of an ongoing project, already has a name: *transduction.* The term reflects an intellectual approach toward a possible object, which we can employ alongside the more conventional activities of deduction and induction. The concept of an urban society, which I introduced above, thus implies a hypothesis and a definition.

Similarly, by "urban revolution" I refer to the transformations that affect contemporary society, ranging from the period when questions of growth and industrialization predominate (models, plans, programs) to the period when the urban problematic becomes predominant, when the search for solutions and modalities unique to urban society are foremost. Some of these transformations are sudden; others are gradual, planned, determined. But which ones? This is a legitimate question. It is by no means certain in advance that the answer will be clear, intellectually satisfying, or unambiguous. The words "urban revolution" do not in themselves refer to actions that are violent. Nor do they exclude them.

But how do we discriminate between the outcome of violent action and the product of rational action before their occurrence? Isn't violence characterized by its ability to spin out of control? Isn't thought characterized by the effort to reduce violence, beginning with the effort to destroy the chains that bind our thought?

There are two aspects of urbanism that we will need to address:

1. For years scholars have viewed urbanism as a social practice that is fundamentally scientific and technical in nature. In this case, theory can and should address this practice by raising it to a conceptual level and, more specifically, to the level of *epistemology*. However, the absence of any such urban epistemology is striking. Is it worth developing such an epistemology, then? No. In fact, its absence is highly significant. For the *institutional* and *ideological* nature of what is referred to as urbanism has—until a new order comes into being—taken precedence over its scientific nature. If we assume that this procedure can be generalized and that understanding always involves epistemology, then it is clear that it plays no role in contemporary urbanism. It is important to understand why and how.

2. As it currently exists, that is, as a policy (having institutional and ideological components), urbanism can be criticized both from the right and the left. The critique from the right, which is well known, is focused on the past and is frequently humanist. It subsumes and justifies a neoliberal ideology of "free enterprise," directly or indirectly. It opens a path for the various "private" initiatives of capitalists and capital. The critique from the left, frequently overlooked, is not associated with any so-called leftist group, club, party, apparatus, or ideology. Rather, it attempts to open a path to the possible, to explore and

delineate a landscape that is not merely part of the "r₍
the accomplished, occupied by existing social, political,
and economic forces. It is a *utopian* critique because it
steps back from the real without, however, losing sight
of it.

We can draw an axis as follows:

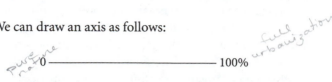

The axis runs from the complete absence of urbanization
("pure nature," the earth abandoned to the elements) on the
left to the completion of the process on the right. A signifier
for this signified—the *urban* (the urban reality)—this axis
is both spatial and temporal: spatial because the process
extends through space, which it modifies; temporal because
it develops over time. Temporality, initially of secondary
importance, eventually becomes the predominant aspect of
practice and history. This schema presents no more than an
aspect of this history, a division of time that is both abstract
and arbitrary and gives rise to operations (periodizations)
that have no absolute privilege but are as necessary (relative)
as other divisions.

I'd like to plant a few signposts along this path delineated
by the "urban phenomenon" (the urban, in short). Initially
there were populations that had been identified by anthropology and ethnology. Around this initial zero, the first
human groups (gatherers, fishers, hunters, possibly herders)
marked out and named space; they explored it while marking it. They indicated place-names, fundamental topoi. It
was a topology and spatial grid that peasants, attached to the
soil, later perfected and refined without upsetting the overall fabric. What is important is that in many places around
the world, and most certainly any place with a history, the
existence of the city has accompanied or followed that of

the village. The representation according to which cultivated land, the village, and farm civilization slowly secreted urban reality reflects an ideology. It generalizes from what took place in Europe during the breakdown of the Roman Empire and following the reconstruction of the medieval city. It's just as easy to maintain the contrary position, however. Agriculture was little more than gathering, and was only formalized through pressure (authoritarian) from the urban centers, generally occupied by skillful conquerors who had become protectors, exploiters, and oppressors, that is, administrators, the founders of a state, or the rudiments of a state. The *political city* accompanies or closely follows the establishment of organized social life, agriculture, and the village.

It goes without saying that such an assumption is meaningless when it involves endless spaces characterized by a seminomadic existence, an impoverished itinerant agriculture. It is obviously based primarily on studies and documents concerning "Asian modes of production," the ancient civilizations that created both urban and agricultural life (Mesopotamia, Egypt, and so on).[1] The general question of the relationship between the city and the countryside is far from being resolved, however.

I'm going to take the risk of locating the *political city* at the point of origin on the space-time axis. The political city was populated primarily by priests, warriors, princes, "nobles," and military leaders, but administrators and scribes were also present. The political city is inconceivable without writing: documents, laws, inventories, tax collection. It is completely given over to orders and decrees, to power. Yet it also implies the existence of exchange to procure the materials essential to warfare and power (metal, leather, and so on), and of artisanship to fashion and maintain them. Thus, such a city also comprises artisans and workers. The political city administers, protects, and exploits a territory that is often vast. It manages large-scale agricultural projects such as drainage, irrigation, the construction of dams, the clearing of land. It rules over a number of villages. Ownership of the land becomes the eminent right of a monarch, the symbol of order and action. Nonetheless, peasants and communities retain effective possession through the payment of tribute.

In such an environment, exchange and trade can only expand. Initially confined to suspicious individuals, to "strangers," they become *functionally* integrated into the life of the city. Those places given over to exchange and trade are initially strongly marked by the signs of *heterotopy*. Like the people who are responsible for and inhabit them, these places are at the outset excluded from the political city: caravansaries, fairgrounds, suburbs. This process of integrating markets and merchandise (people and things) in the city can last for centuries. Exchange and trade, which are essential to the survival of life, bring wealth and movement. The political city resists this with all the power at its disposal, all its cohesiveness; it feels, knows, that it is threatened by markets, merchandise, and traders, by their form of ownership (money, a form of personal property, being movable by definition). There is ample evidence that Athens, a political city, coexisted with Piraeus, a commercial city, and that attempts to ban the presence of merchandise in the agora, a free space and political meeting place, were unsuccessful. When Christ chased the merchants from the temple, the ban was similar, had the same meaning. In China and Japan, merchants were for years an urban underclass, relegated to a "special" (heterotopic) part of the city. In truth, it is only in the European West, at the end of the Middle Ages, that merchandise, the market, and merchants were able to successfully penetrate the city. Prior to this, itinerant merchants—part warrior, part thief—deliberately chose to remain in the fortified remains of ancient (Roman) cities to facilitate their struggle against the territorial lords. Based on this assumption, the renewed political city would have served as a frame for the action that was to transform it. During this (class) struggle against the overlords, who were the owners and rulers of the territory, a prodigiously fecund struggle in the West that helped create not only a history but history itself, the marketplace became centralized. It replaced and supplanted the place of assembly (the agora, the forum). Around the market, which had now become an essential part of the city, were grouped the church and town hall (occupied by a merchant oligarchy), with its belfry or campanile, the symbol of liberty. Architecture follows and translates the new conception of the city. Urban space becomes the meeting place for goods and people, for exchange. It bears the signs of this conquered liberty, which is perceived as Liberty—a grandiose but hopeless struggle. In this sense, it is legitimate to assign a symbolic value to the *bastides,* or walled towns, of southwest France, the first cities to take shape around the local marketplace. History is filled with irony. The fetishism associated with merchandise appeared along with the rise of merchandise, its logic and ideology, its language and world. In the fourteenth century it was believed that it was sufficient to establish a market and build stores, gateways, and galleries around a central square to promote the growth of goods and buyers. In this way, both the nobility and the bourgeoisie built merchant cities in areas that were undeveloped, practically desert, and still crisscrossed by herds and migratory, seminomadic tribes. These cities of the French southwest, although they bear the names of some of our great and wealthy cities (Barcelona, Bologna, Plaisance, Florence, Grenada, and so on), were failures. The *merchant city* succeeded the political city. At this time (approximately the fourteenth century in western Europe), commercial exchange became an urban *function,* which was embodied in a *form* (or forms, both architectural and urban). This in turn gave urban space a new *structure.* The changes that took place in Paris illustrate this complex

interaction among the three essential aspects of function, form, and structure. Market towns and suburbs, which were initially commercial and artisanal—Beaubourg, Saint-Antoine, Saint-Honoré—grew in importance and began to struggle with centers of political power (institutions) for influence, prestige, and space, forcing them to compromise, entering with them in the construction of a powerful urban unity.

At one moment in the history of the European West, an event of great importance occurred, but one that remained latent because it went unnoticed. The importance of the city for the social whole became such that the whole seemed to shift. In the relationship between town and country, the emphasis was still on the countryside: real property wealth, the products of the soil, attachment to the land (owners of fiefs or noble titles). Compared with the countryside, the town retained its heterotopic character, marked by its ramparts as well as the transition to suburban areas. At a given moment, these various relationships were reversed; the situation changed. The moment when this shift occurred, this reversal of heterotopy, should be marked along our axis. From this moment on, the city would no longer appear as an urban island in a rural ocean, it would no longer seem a paradox, a monster, a hell or heaven that contrasted sharply with village or country life in a natural environment. It entered people's awareness and understanding as one of the terms in the opposition between town and country. Country? It is now no more than—nothing more than—the town's "environment," its horizon, its limit. Villagers? As far as they were concerned, they no longer worked for the territorial lords, they produced for the city, for the urban market. And even though they realized that the wheat and wood merchants exploited them, they understood that the path to freedom crossed the marketplace.

So what is happening around this crucial moment in history? Thoughtful people no longer see themselves reflected in nature, a shadowy world subject to mysterious forces. Between them and nature, between their home (the focal point of thought, existence) and the world, lies the urban reality, an essential mediating factor. From this moment on society no longer coincides with the countryside. It no longer coincides with the city, either. The state encompasses them both, joins them in its hegemony by making use of their rivalry. Yet, at the time, the majesty of the state was veiled to its contemporaries. Of whom or what was Reason an attribute? Royalty? Divine right? The individual? Yet this is what led to the reform of the city after the destruction of Athens and Rome, after the most important products of those civilizations, logic and law, were lost from view. The logos was reborn, but its rebirth was not attributed to the renaissance of the urban world but to transcendent reason. The rationalism that culminated in Descartes accompanied the reversal that replaced the primacy of the peasantry with the priority of urban life. Although the peasantry didn't see it as such. However, during this period, the *image of the city* came into being.

The city had writing; it had secrets and powers, and clarified the opposition between urbanity (cultured) and rusticity (naive and brutal). After a certain point in time, the city developed its own form of writing: the map or *plan*, the science of *planimetry*. During the sixteenth and seventeenth centuries, when this reversal of meaning took place, maps of European cities began to appear, including the first maps of the city of Paris. These are not yet abstract maps, projections of urban space onto geometric coordinates. A cross between vision and concept, works of art and science, they displayed the city from top to bottom, in perspective, painted, depicted, and geometrically described. This perspective, simultaneously idealist and realist—the perspective of thought and power—was situated in the vertical dimension, the dimension of knowledge and reason, and dominated and constituted a totality: the city. This shift of social reality toward the urban, this (relative) discontinuity, can be easily indicated on a space-time axis, whose continuity can be used to situate and date any (relative) breaks. All that is needed is to draw a line between the zero point and the terminal point (which I'll assume to be one hundred).

This reversal of meaning can't be dissociated from the growth of commercial capital and the existence of the market. It was the rise of the mercantile city, which was grafted onto the political city but promoted its own ascendancy, that was primarily responsible. This was soon followed by the appearance of industrial capital and, consequently, the *industrial city*. This requires further explanation. Was industry associated with the city? One would assume it to be associated with the *non-city*, the absence or rupture of urban reality. We know that industry initially developed near the sources of energy (coal and water), raw materials (metals, textiles), and manpower reserves. Industry gradually made its way into the city in search of capital and capitalists, markets, and an abundant supply of low-cost labor. It could locate itself anywhere, therefore, but sooner or later made its way into existing cities or created new cities, although it was prepared to move elsewhere if there was an economic advantage in doing so. Just as the political city resisted the conquest—half-pacific, half-violent—of the merchants, exchange, and money, similarly the political and mercantile city defended itself from being taken over by a nascent industry, industrial capital, and capital itself. But how did it do this? Through corporatism, by establishing relationships. Historical continuity and evolution mask the effects and ruptures associated with such transitions. Yet something strange and wonderful was also taking place, which helped renew dialectical thought: the non-city and the anti-city would conquer the city, penetrate it, break it apart, and in so doing extend it immeasurably, bringing about the urbanization of society and the growth of the urban fabric that covered what was left of the city prior to the arrival of industry. This extraordinary movement has escaped our attention and has been described in piecemeal fashion because ideologues have tried to eliminate dialectical thought and the analysis of contradictions in favor of logical thought—that is, the identification of coherence and nothing but coherence. Urban reality, simultaneously amplified and exploded, thus loses the features it inherited from the previous period: organic totality, belonging, an uplifting image, a sense of space that was measured and dominated by monumental splendor. It was populated with signs of the urban within the dissolution of urbanity; it became stipulative, repressive, marked by signals, summary codes for circulation (routes), and signage. It was sometimes read as a rough draft, sometimes as an authoritarian message. It was imperious. But none of these descriptive terms completely describes the historical process of implosion-explosion (a metaphor borrowed from nuclear physics) that occurred: the tremendous concentration (of people, activities, wealth, goods, objects, instruments, means, and thought) of urban reality and the immense explosion, the projection of numerous, disjunct fragments (peripheries, suburbs, vacation homes, satellite towns) into space.

The *industrial city* (often a shapeless town, a barely urban agglomeration, a conglomerate, or conurbation like the Ruhr Valley) serves as a prelude to a *critical zone*. At this moment, the effects of implosion-explosion are most fully felt. The increase in industrial production is superimposed on the growth of commercial exchange and multiplies the number of such exchanges. This growth extends from simple barter to the global market, from the simple exchange between two individuals all the way to the exchange of products, works of art, ideas, and human beings. Buying and selling, merchandise and market, money and capital appear to sweep away all obstacles. During this period of generalization, the effect of the process—namely the urban reality—becomes both cause and reason. Induced factors become dominant (inductors). The *urban problematic* becomes a global phenomenon. Can urban reality be defined as a "superstructure" on the surface of the economic structure, whether capitalist or socialist? The simple result of growth and productive forces? Simply a modest marginal reality compared with production? Not at all. Urban reality modifies the relations of production without being sufficient to transform them. It becomes a productive force, like science. Space and the politics of space "express" social relationships but react against them. Obviously, if an urban reality manifests itself and becomes dominant, it does so only through the urban problematic. What can be done to change this? How can we build cities or "something" that replaces what was formerly the City? How can we reconceptualize the urban phenomenon? How can we formulate, classify, and order the innumerable questions that arise, questions that move, although not without considerable resistance, to the forefront of our awareness? Can we achieve significant progress in theory and practice so that our consciousness can comprehend a reality that overflows it and a possible that flees before its grasp?

We can represent this process as follows:

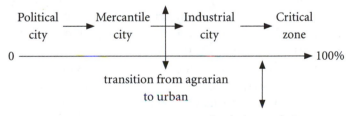

| Political city | Mercantile city | Industrial city | Critical zone |

0 ————————————————————→ 100%

transition from agrarian
to urban

implosion-explosion
(urban concentration, rural
exodus, extension of the urban
fabric, complete subordination of
the agrarian to the urban)

What occurs during the *critical phase?* This book is an attempt to answer that question, which situates the urban problematic within the overall process. Are the theoretical assumptions that enable us to draw an axis such as the one shown above, introduce directed time, and make sense of the critical zone sufficient to help us understand what is taking place? Possibly. In any event, there are several assumptions we can make now. Lacking any proof to the contrary, we can postulate that a second transition occurs, a second reversal of direction and situation. Industrialization, the dominant power and limiting factor, becomes a dominated reality during periods of profound crisis. This results in tremendous confusion, during which the past and the possible, the best and the worst, become intertwined.

In spite of this theoretical hypothesis concerning the possible and its relation to the actual (the "real"), we should not overlook the fact that the onset of urban society and the modalities of urbanization depend on the characteristics of society as it existed during the course of industrialization (neocapitalist or socialist, full economic growth or intense automation). The onset of urban society at different times, the implications and consequences of these initial differences, are part of the problematic associated with the urban phenomenon, or simply the "urban." These terms are preferable to the word "city," which appears to designate a clearly defined, definitive *object,* a scientific object and the immediate goal of action, whereas the theoretical approach requires a critique of this "object" and a more complex notion of the virtual or possible object. Within this perspective there is no science of the city (such as urban sociology or urban economy), but an emerging understanding of the overall process, as well as its term (goal and direction).

The urban (an abbreviated form of urban society) can therefore be defined not as an accomplished reality, situated behind the actual in time, but, on the contrary, as a horizon, an illuminating virtuality. It is the possible, defined by a direction, that moves toward the urban as the culmination of its journey. To reach it—in other words, to realize it—we must first overcome or break through the obstacles that currently make it *impossible*. Can theoretical knowledge treat this virtual object, the goal of action, as an abstraction? No. From this point on, it is abstract only in the sense that it is a *scientific*, and therefore legitimate, abstraction. Theoretical knowledge can and must reveal the terrain, the foundation on which it resides: an ongoing social practice, an urban practice in the process of formation. It is an aspect of the critical phase that this practice is currently veiled and disjointed, that it possesses only fragments of a reality and a science that are still in the future. It is our job to demonstrate that such an approach has an outcome, that there are solutions to the current problematic. The *virtual object* is nothing but planetary society and the "global city," and it stands outside the global and planetary crisis of reality and thought, outside the old borders that had been drawn when agriculture was dominant and that were maintained during the growth of exchange and industrial production. Nevertheless, the urban problematic can't absorb every problem. There are problems that are unique to agriculture and industry, even though the urban reality modifies them. Moreover, the urban problematic requires that we exercise considerable caution when exploring the realm of the possible. It is the analyst's responsibility to identify and describe the various forms of urbanization and explain what happens to the forms, functions, and urban structures that are transformed by the breakup of the ancient city and the process of generalized urbanization. Until now the critical phase was perceived as a kind of black box. We know what enters the box, and sometimes we see what comes out, but we don't know what goes on inside. This makes conventional procedures of forecasting and projection useless, since they extrapolate from the actual, from a set of facts. Projections and forecasts have a determined basis only in the fragmentary sciences: demography, for example, or political economy. But what is at stake here, "objectively," is a totality.

To illustrate the depth of the crisis, the uncertainty and perplexity that accompany the critical phase, an element of contrast may be useful. Is this merely a question of style? Yes, but not entirely. Here, I would like to introduce the pros and cons of streets and monuments. I'll leave other issues— nature, the city, urbanism, the urban—for later.

For the street. The street is more than just a place for movement and circulation. The invasion of the automobile and the pressure of the automobile lobby have turned the car into a key object, parking into an obsession, traffic into a priority, harmful to urban and social life. The day is approaching when we will be forced to limit the rights and powers of the automobile. Naturally, this won't be easy, and the fallout will be considerable. What about the street, however? It serves as a meeting place (topos), for without it no other designated encounters are possible (cafés, theaters, halls). These places animate the street and are served by its animation, or they cease to exist. In the street, a form of spontaneous theater, I become spectacle and spectator, and sometimes an actor. The street is where movement takes place, the interaction without which urban life would not exist, leaving only separation, a forced and fixed segregation. And there are consequences to eliminating the street (ever since Le Corbusier and his *nouveaux ensembles*): the extinction of life, the reduction of the city to a dormitory, the aberrant functionalization of existence. The street contains functions that were overlooked by Le Corbusier: the informative function, the symbolic function, the ludic function. The street is a place to play and learn. The street is disorder. All the elements of urban life, which are fixed and redundant elsewhere, are free to fill the streets and through the streets flow to the centers, where they meet and interact, torn from their fixed abode. This disorder is alive. It informs. It surprises. The work of Jane Jacobs has shown that, in the United States, the street (highly trafficked, busy) provides the only security possible against criminal violence (theft, rape, aggression). Wherever streets disappeared, criminality increased, became organized. In the street and through the space it offered, a group (the city itself) took shape, appeared, appropriated places, realized an appropriated space-time. This appropriation demonstrates that use and use value can dominate exchange and exchange value.

Revolutionary events generally take place in the street. Doesn't this show that the disorder of the street engenders another kind of order? The urban space of the street is a place for talk, given over as much to the exchange of words and signs as it is to the exchange of things. A place where speech becomes writing. A place where speech can become "savage" and, by escaping rules and institutions, inscribe itself on walls.

Against the street. A meeting place? Maybe, but such meetings are superficial. In the street, we merely brush shoulders with others, we don't interact with them. It's the "we" that is important. The street prevents the constitution of a group, a subject; it is populated by a congeries of people in search of . . . of what exactly? The world of merchandise is deployed in the street. The merchandise that didn't make it into specialized locales or markets (marketplaces, halls) has invaded the entire city. In antiquity the streets were merely extensions of places with specialized functions: the temple, the stadium, the agora, the garden. During the Middle Ages, artisans occupied the streets. The artisan was both producer and seller. The artisans were followed by merchants, who, although only merchants, soon became masters. The street became a display, a corridor flanked by stores of various kinds. Merchandise became spectacle (provocative, attractive) and transformed the individual into a spectacle for others. Here, more than elsewhere, exchange and exchange value take precedence over use, reducing it to a residue. Therefore, the critique of the street must be more incisive: the street becomes the focus of a form of repression that was made possible by the "real"—that is, weak, alienated, and alienating—character of the relationships that are formed there. Movement in the street, a communications space, is both obligatory and repressed. Whenever threatened, the first thing power restricts is the ability to linger or assemble in the street. Although the street may have once had the meaning of a meeting place, it has since lost it, and could only have lost it, by reducing itself, through a process of necessary reduction, to nothing more than a passageway, by splitting itself into a place for the passage of pedestrians (hunted) and automobiles (privileged). The street became a network organized for and by consumption. The rate of pedestrian circulation, although still tolerated, was determined and measured by the ability to perceive store windows and buy the objects displayed in them. Time became "merchandise time" (time for buying and selling, time bought and sold). The street regulated time outside of work; it subjected it to the same system, the system of yield and profit. It was nothing more than the necessary transition between forced labor, programmed leisure, and habitation as a place of consumption.

In the street, the neocapitalist organization of consumption is demonstrated by its power, which is not restricted to political power or repression (overt or covert). The street, a series of displays, an exhibition of objects for sale, illustrates just how the logic of merchandise is accompanied by a form of (passive) contemplation that assumes the appearance and significance of an aesthetics and an ethics. The accumulation of objects accompanies the growth of population and capital; it is transformed into an ideology, which, dissimulated beneath the traits of the legible and visible, comes to seem self-evident. In this sense we can speak of a *colonization* of the urban space, which takes place in the street through the image, through publicity, through the spectacle of objects— a "system of objects" that has become symbol and spectacle. Through the uniformization of the grid, visible in the modernization of old streets, objects (merchandise) take on the effects of color and form that make them attractive. The parades, masquerades, balls, and folklore festivals authorized by a power structure caricaturize the appropriation and reappropriation of space. The true appropriation characteristic of effective "demonstrations" is challenged by the forces of repression, which demand silence and forgetfulness.

Against the monument. The monument is essentially repressive. It is the seat of an institution (the church, the state, the university). Any space that is organized around the monument is colonized and oppressed. The great monuments have been raised to glorify conquerors and the powerful. Occasionally they glorify the dead or the beauty of death (the Taj Mahal) in palaces and tombs. The misfortune of architecture is that it wanted to construct monuments, but the idea of *habiting* them was either conceived in terms of those monuments or neglected entirely.[2] The extension of monumental space to habiting is always catastrophic, and for the most part hidden from those who are subject to it. Monumental splendor is formal. And although the monument is always laden with symbols, it presents them to social awareness and contemplation (passive) just when those symbols, already outdated, are beginning to lose their meaning, such as the symbols of the revolution on the Napoleonic Arc de Triomphe.

For the monument. It is the only conceivable or imaginable site of collective (social) life. It controls people, yes, but does so to bring them together. Beauty and monumentality go hand in hand. The great monuments were transfunctional (cathedrals) and even transcultural (tombs). This is what gave them their ethical and aesthetic power. Monuments project onto the land a conception of the world, whereas the city projected (and continues to project) social life (globality). In their very essence, and sometimes at the very heart of a space in which the characteristics of a society are most recognizable and commonplace, monuments embody a sense of transcendence, a sense of being *elsewhere*. They have always been u-topic. Throughout their height and depth, along a dimension that was alien to urban trajectories, they proclaimed duty, power, knowledge, joy, hope.

2 || Blind Field

virtual object

In this book I have not, for the most part, followed the historical method as it is generally understood. Superficially it may appear that I have been describing and analyzing the genesis of the city as object and its modifications and transformations. But my initial concern has been with a virtual object, which I have used to describe a space-time axis. The future illuminates the past, the virtual allows us to examine and situate the realized. The breakdown of the preindustrialist and precapitalist city caused by the impact of industry and capitalism helps us understand the conditions and antecedents of the industrial city. Its predecessor, the mercantile city, in turn enables us to comprehend the political city on which it was superimposed. Marx believed that adulthood comprises the child as subject (awareness) and enables us to understand its point of departure, the rough form that may be richer and more complex than the adult, as a real object. And it is bourgeois society, however complex and opaque it might be, that allows us to understand the most transparent societies, ancient and medieval society. Not the opposite. With the arrival of time and historicity, our awareness is able to grasp two opposing movements: *regressive* (from the virtual to the actual, the actual to the past) and *progressive* (from the obsolete and completed to the movement that anticipates that completeness, that presages and brings into being something new).

Historical time can be broken down (periodized) by mode of production: Asiatic, slave, feudal, capitalist, socialist. This breakdown has certain advantages and certain disadvantages. When pushed too far, when we emphasize the divisions, the internal character of each mode of production, the consistency of each mode as a totality, the transition between them becomes unintelligible at the very moment when their individual intelligibility becomes most evident. Moreover, each mode of production has "produced" (not in the sense of any ordinary thing but as a privileged work) a type of city, which "expresses" it in a way that is immediately visible and legible on the environment, by making the most abstract relationships—legal, political, ideological—tangible. This discontinuous aspect of time cannot be pushed so far as to make continuity unintelligible. A relatively continuous cumulative process is also at work in the city: the accumulation of knowledge, technologies, things, people, wealth, money, and capital. The city is where this accumulation occurs, even though capital may arise from wealth that has been created in the countryside and even though industrial investment may be detrimental to the city.

The Marxist theory of surplus value distinguishes the formation of surplus value from its realization and distribution. Surplus value is initially formed in the countryside. This formation is shifted to the city to the extent that it becomes the center of production, craft activities, and industry. In contrast, the commercial and banking system found in cities has always been an organ for the realization of surplus value. In distributing wealth, those who controlled the city have also attempted to retain the majority of this surplus value (greater than the average profit from their investments). For these three aspects of surplus value, the urban center plays an increasingly important role, an aspect of urban centrality that is essential yet misunderstood (unnoticed) within the mode of capitalist production. This contradicts the belief that the city of old and the contemporary urban center were no more than superstructures and had no relation to productive forces and the mode of production.

The space-time axis can be used to situate both certain relationships between city and country and their transformations. It neither reflects nor contains all of them. For example, it contains neither the conditions nor the elements of concepts associated with those relationships: nature (physis) and logos (reason). It fails to reveal the genealogy of the idea of Nature and its development. The diagram in chapter 1 indicates a reversal within European history at a moment that is currently referred to as the Renaissance. What happened exactly to the concepts and representations designated by the terms "nature" and "reason" during this critical phase? Because the relationship between city and country was profoundly altered, was there any correspondence or distortion between these alterations and the alteration of the associated concepts? Can the unique polysemy of "nature" and "reason" be analyzed and explained on the basis of history given above? Possibly. Why did the fetishism of nature occur at the end of the eighteenth and beginning of the nineteenth century? What did it mean? Wasn't there a twofold negation of nature, as something prior to thought and "human" action, a twofold negation by the city and by industry, which once again exposed and mirrored nature? From this moment on, the City appeared as a second nature of stone and metal, built on an initial, fundamental nature made of earth, air, water, and fire. This second nature acquired its paradigm, its system of pertinent oppositions—light and dark, water and stone, tree and metal, monstrous and paradisiac, rough and polished, savage and artificial—in and through the poets (Hugo, Baudelaire). This in turn refers us back to the myths of the city, which I'll discuss below. But what becomes of the attempt, inherent in urban space, to reunite the spontaneous and the artificial, nature and culture? There is no city, no urban space without a garden or park, without the simulation of nature, without labyrinths, the evocation of the ocean or forest, without trees tormented into strange human and inhuman shapes. What can be said, then, about the gardens and parks that are just as responsible for the quality of urban life in Paris, London, Tokyo, and New York as their squares and network of streets? Are these spaces the site of a term-for-term correspondence, or nearly so, between the city and the country? Could they be the visible re-presentation of an *elsewhere*, the utopia of nature? Do they provide an essential reference point against which urban reality can situate and perceive itself? Or are they only a neutral element of the urban agglomeration? What happens to these functions (multifunctional or transfunctional realities) in these "open spaces"? Wasn't the problem resolved, arbitrarily and without awareness, by this neutralization of unbuilt space, with its illusory devotion to a fictive nature, to "open space"?

These aspects of the urban problematic (which are not minor and are more insightful than the commonplace images of the "environment" because they imply an analysis of some sort) do not appear in the diagram. However, they are part of the critical phase, which contains them. Depending on the metaphor used, we can say that this phase is a *blank* (a void) or a dark moment (a "black box"), or that it designates a *blind field*. During the critical phase, nature appears as one of the key problems. Industrialization and urbanization, together or in competition, ravage nature. Water, earth, air, fire—the elements—are threatened with destruction. By the year 2000, whether or not there has been nuclear war, our water and air will be so polluted that life on earth will be difficult to maintain. It is now possible to conceive of a form of

problematic concerning nature

Blind Field || 27

"socialism" that differs considerably from what is commonly understood by the word or from what Marx defined. Goods that were once scarce are now abundant, such as bread and food in general (which are still scarce in a large, poorly developed, part of the world, but superabundant in the developed part). In contrast, goods that were once abundant have become scarce: space, time, desire, water, earth, light. Unless we intend to produce or re-produce everything that was "nature," we will have to collectively manage new types of scarcity.

The partial problematic concerning "nature" can be determined in this way. Theoretically, nature is shrinking, but the signs of nature and the natural are multiplying, replacing and supplanting real "nature." These signs are mass-produced and sold. A tree, a flower, a branch, a scent, or a word can become signs of absence: of an illusory and fictive presence. At the same time, ideological naturalization becomes obsessive. There is a continuous reference to nature in advertising, whether it be for food or textile products, housing or vacations. To provide meaning and content (illusory), the re-presentation of nature is accompanied by the full range of "floating signifiers" employed by rhetoric. What no longer has a meaning is given one through the mediation of a fetishistic world of nature. Undiscoverable, fugitive, ravaged, the residue of urbanization and industrialization, nature can be found everywhere, from femininity to the most mundane object. Parks and open spaces, the last word in good intentions and bad urban representation, are simply a poor substitute for nature, the degraded simulacrum of the open space characteristic of encounters, games, parks, gardens, and public squares. This space, which has been neutralized by a degrading form of democratization, has as its symbol the square. The urbanist passively obeys the pressures of number and least cost; the functionality he thinks he has created is reduced to an absence of "real" functions, to a function of passive observation.

Critical phase. Black box. The architect and the urbanist,

sometimes confused as partners in an ambiguous duo, sometimes as twins or warring siblings, as distant colleagues and
rivals, examine the black box. They know what goes in, are
amazed at what comes out, but have no idea what takes place
inside. My schema won't help them. For it assumes that the
city (the urban center) has been a place for creation and not
simply a result, the simple spatial effect of a creative act that
occurred elsewhere, in the Mind, or the Intellect. It stipulates
that the urban can become "objective," that is, creation and
creator, meaning and goal.

There are three layers. Three periods. Three "fields." These
are not simply social phenomena but sensations and percep-
tions, spaces and times, images and concepts, language and
rationality, theories and social practices:

- the rural (peasant)
- the industrial
- the urban

They are accompanied by emergences and interferences,
shifts, advances and delays, various inequalities of development. There are painful transitions, critical phases. The
space-time axis reveals a number of highlights or divisions,
so many theoretical assumptions in need of verification.
But what happens between two periods, at the point of
transition between two periods, within the break or fold
(today, between the industrial and the urban)? Verbal layers, detached floating signifiers whose signified (industry,
rationality, and practice) is no longer sufficient, even though
it is necessary. These verbal layers, wandering about their na-
tive soil, are unable to attach themselves to a "philosophical
subject" or a "privileged object" or a "historical totalization."
We can look at them the way we look at various cloud layers
from an airplane. Here, high above the earth, floating lightly,
is the cirrus of ancient philosophy, the nimbus of rationality,

and the heavy cumulus of scientism. They are languages, or metalanguages, halfway between the real and the fictive, between the realized and the possible. They float freely, escaping the incantations of sorcerer philosophers.

Between fields, which are regions of force and conflict, there are *blind fields*. These are not merely dark and uncertain, poorly explored, but blind in the sense that there is a blind spot on the retina, the center—and negation—of vision. A paradox. The eye doesn't see; it needs a mirror. The center of vision doesn't see and doesn't know it is blind. Do these paradoxes extend to thought, to awareness, to knowledge? In the past there was a field between the rural and the industrial—just as there is today between the industrial and the urban—that was invisible to us.

What does our blindness look like? We focus attentively on the new field, the urban, but we see it with eyes, with concepts, that were shaped by the practices and theories of industrialization, with a fragmentary analytic tool that was designed during the industrial period and is therefore *reductive* of the emerging reality. We no longer see that reality; we resist it, turn away from it, struggle against it, prevent its birth and development.

The urban (urban space, urban landscape) remains unseen. *We* still don't see it. Is it simply that our eye has been shaped (misshaped) by the earlier landscape so it can no longer see a new space? Is it that our way of seeing has been cultivated by village spaces, by the bulk of factories, by the monuments of past eras? Yes, but there's more to it than that. It's not just a question of lack of education, but of occlusion. We see things incompletely. How many people perceive "perspective," angles and contours, volumes, straight and curved lines, but are unable to perceive or conceive multiple paths, complex spaces? They are unable to leap over the quotidian, manufactured according to the constraints of industrial production and the consumption of industrial products,

to the urban, which has shaken off those determinisms and constraints. They are unable to construct a landscape, composing and proposing a specifically urban idea of ugliness and beauty. The urban reality, even before its inception and affirmation, is reduced by the rural (garden suburbs, so-called open spaces) and by the industrial quotidian (functional units of habitation, neighborhoods, relations, monotonous but required routes), an *everydayness* that is subject to the requirements of the enterprise and treated in accordance with corporate rationality. This involves a reduction that is both social and mental, toward trivialization and toward specialization. In a word, the urban is reduced to the industrial. Blindness, our not-seeing and not-knowing, implies an ideology. These blind fields embed themselves in re-presentation. Initially, we are faced with a *presentation* of the facts and groups of facts, a way of perceiving and grouping. This is followed by a *re-presentation*, an interpretation of the facts. Between these two moments and in each of them, there are misrepresentations, misunderstandings. The blinding (assumptions we accept dogmatically) and the blinded (the misunderstood) are complementary aspects of our blindness.

The notion of a blind field is neither a literary image nor a metaphor, in spite of the paradox of combining a subjective term "blind" and an objective term "field" (which, moreover, is always thought of as being illuminated). There are several ways to elucidate the concept, which can be approached both philosophically and scientifically; that is, as a result of philosophical analysis and through the understanding.[1] This concept has nothing to do with the trivial distinction between shadow and light, even if we add to this the fact that intellectual "illumination" has its limits, pushes aside or ignores some things, projects itself in certain places and not others, brackets certain pieces of information and highlights others. In addition, there are things we don't know and things we are unable to explain.

What we find in a blind field is insignificant, but given meaning through research. Was sex significant before Freud? Yes. Sin and shame were part of Western (Judeo-Christian) culture. As were ideal patterns in poetry, for certain poets at least. Giving these things a meaning was an act. Before Freud, sex was isolated, torn apart, reduced, rejected (repressed). It passed through a blind field, populated with shadows and phantoms, driven back from any concrete identity under unrelenting pressure, some fundamental alienation. Nothing was better suited to a "mystical chiaroscuro."

Is the unconscious the substance or essence of a blind field? Remember, these are fields and open to exploration: for the understanding they are virtuality, for action they are possibility. How and why are they blind? Bad faith, misunderstanding, and a failure of recognition (false awareness and possibly false consciousness) play a role. It would be more accurate therefore to speak of the unrecognized than the unconscious. However, these terms are unsatisfactory. Why do "I" (or "we") refuse to see, perceive, or conceive something? Why do we pretend not to see? How do we arrive at that point? There are undeveloped regions (unappropriated) of the body, including sex. However, these blind fields are both mental and social. To understand them, we must take into account the power of ideology (which illuminates other fields or brings fictional fields into view) and the power of language. There are "blind fields" whenever language fails us, whenever there is surfeit or redundancy in a metalanguage (discourse about discourse, signifiers floating far from their signifieds).

This brings us back to the contrast between the blinding and the blinded. The blinding is the luminous source (knowledge or ideology) that projects a beam of light, that illuminates *elsewhere*. The blinded is our dazed stare, as well as the region left in shadow. On the one hand a path is opened to exploration; on the other there is an enclosure to break out of, a consecration to transgress.

Three fields or domains. We can express this as the discovery, emergence, and constitution, or historic creation, of three continents: the agrarian, industrial, and urban. This is analogous to the discovery of mathematics, followed by physics, followed by history and society in the process of understanding, a succession acknowledged by epistemology. However, within this succession, there are no "ruptures" as contemporary epistemology understands the term. Not only are there simultaneities, interactions, or inequalities of development through which these moments (these "continents") can coexist, not only would such a notion of "rupture" cast into darkness relations of class and production, but so-called underdeveloped countries are now characterized by the fact that they undergo the rural, the industrial, and the urban simultaneously. They accumulate problems without accumulating wealth. We can also say that these moments correspond to the tripartite division that is found, although with a slightly different emphasis, in every social practice: need, work, enjoyment. *Need* would correspond to the agrarian period, one of limited production, subject to "nature" and interspersed with catastrophe and famine, a domain of scarcity. *Work* would correspond to the industrial period, one of fetishized productivity and the destruction of nature, including the nature that lives or survives in a human being. Would *enjoyment* correspond to urban society? It remains to be seen.

Three fields. These do not reflect a given historical, economic, or sociological approach, but a (doubly) global concept: a succession of periods and those periods taken individually. The term "field" does not refer only to successive or superimposed layers of facts or phenomena, but also to modes of thought, action, and life.

The "rural-peasant" field, for example, comprises a representation of space or, another way of putting it, a spatial grid that implies orientation, marking, and the ability to grasp sites and name places (place-names, topoi in defined spaces that are attached to particularities of "nature"). It assumes a form of spontaneity that is highly constrained by the incessant action of a community. This cannot occur without mental and social particularities, without an originality that results from a group's origin (ethnicity, climate, geographical framework, "natural" production modified by agricultural activities, etc.). The particularities of such groups find their primary expression in the confluence of two activities that are distinct yet tendentiously opposite: magic and religion. They require priests and sorcerers. Through their joint operation, the simple cycles and rhythms (days, seasons, years) take place within the great cosmic cycles. An immediate thought, which is also a thought of the immediate (that which takes place here and now, what needs to be done today or tomorrow), is integrated within a much more expansive way of thinking that encompasses entire lifetimes and the events in those lifetimes—births, marriages, deaths, funerals—as well as the succession of generations. Sorcerers dispose of the immediate; priests take care of the world at large. The rural-peasant, although primordial and a dominant field for centuries, only took shape after being acted upon by its conquerors, by administrators in the political city. Such cities can have only a political existence, dominating a rural world whose rivers bathe, nourish, and occasionally submerge it. The political city is not yet urban. It is barely a presentiment. Still, even though the political city is as well established as the peasant communities and is strongly marked by that environment, the (fundamental) division of labor between the two fragments of society has already taken shape. The distinction between the city and the country becomes associated with other oppositions that will develop in time: material and intellectual labor, production and trade, agriculture and industry. These oppositions are initially complementary, then virtually contradictory, then conflicting. The countryside corresponds to forms of land ownership (real property) that are tribal and later feudal. The city corresponds to other types of property: movable (initially hardly distinct from real property), artisanal, then capitalist. During this prehistory, elements and forms come together that will later become history, breaking apart and combating one another.

The industrial field replaces natural, or presumably natural, particularities with a methodically and systematically imposed homogeneity. This is done in the name of reason, law, authority, technology, the state, the class that holds hegemonic power. All the elements are in place to legitimize and establish a general order that follows the logic of commodities, the "world" of commodities realized on a global scale by capitalism and the bourgeoisie. It has sometimes been asked whether socialism can circumvent the reign of political economy. This project of generalized rationality literally creates a void before it. It destroys mentally before it destroys through its efficiency. It creates a blind field because it is barren. Just what does this *project* for universal rationality consist in? It extends to all activities what began as an experiment, namely, the industrial division of labor. Within the enterprise, labor is divided up and organized so it can be completed without the products of that labor or the labor itself passing through the marketplace. The greatest challenge to the industrial era, a project that has been undertaken repeatedly but never accomplished, has been to extend the efficiency of industrial division to the social division of labor. The social division of labor has been intensified (without, however, ever being rationally organized) until it is nothing more than the dusty remains of separate activities. This applies to both materially productive labor and unproductive but socially necessary labor (intellectual, scientific). Analytic fragmentation becomes so intense that the unity (synthesis) supposedly supplied by a dominant religion, philosophy, state, or science is artificially superimposed on the dust of "disciplines," laws, and facts. The general, that is spatio-temporal, organization of social practice has the appearance of being completely rational because it is constructed from order and constraint. The homogeneous space-time that practice attempts to realize and totalize is filled with the dust of objects, fragmented activities, situations, and people in situations, a congeries whose coherence is only apparent, especially since such appearance makes use of imperious systematization.

There is indeed something suspect in the "industrial city." Does it exist? In this sense, yes. In another sense, no. It is a phantom, a shadow of urban reality, a spectral analysis of dispersed and external elements that have been reunited through constraint. Several *logics* meet head-on and sometimes clash: the logic of commodities (stretched so far as to attempt to organize production on the basis of consumption), the logic of the state and the law, the organization of space (town and country planning and urbanism), the logic of the object, of daily life, language, information, communication. Because each logic wants to be restrictive and complete, eliminating anything that is felt to be unsuitable, claiming to govern the remainder of the world, it becomes an empty tautology. In this way, communication only transmits the communicable. But all these logics and all these tautologies confront one another at some point. They share a common space: the logic of surplus value. The city, or what remains of it or what it will become, is better suited than it has ever been for the accumulation of capital; that is, the accumulation, realization, and distribution of surplus value. However, these logics and tautologies deny nature. There is nothing abstract about this negation, nothing speculative. By rejecting particularity, industrial rationality simply ravages nature and everything associated with "naturalism." This results in obsession, a second state of awareness, thought, and language.

Analytic thought, which claims to be a form of integral rationality (integrating and integrated), requires an intermediary to perform effectively. The reign of rational finality, therefore, changes in importance with the nature of the intermediary. In fact, this rationality follows from a misguided application of organizational processes and operations appropriate to the enterprise. It confides partial tasks to social auxiliaries, who struggle to achieve autonomy: bureaucrats, merchants, publicists, advertisers. Since generalized dislocation and separation are common, a general malaise accompanies the satisfaction obtained from ideology, consumption, and the predominance of the rational. Everything becomes calculable and predictable, quantifiable and transferable. Everything must be part of an order (apparent and fictional) enhanced by constraints—everything except a residue of disorder and freedom, which is sometimes tolerated, sometimes hunted down with overwhelming repressive force. It is during this period that "history" accelerates its course, strips off any particularities, lops off whatever was characterized by privilege or distinction, whether works of art or people. It is a period of warfare and revolution, which abort as soon as they appear to realize themselves in the cult of the state and the fetishism of production, which is itself the realization of the fetishism of money and commodities.

These events are succeeded by the *urban*. I will try to show that this is a new field, still unknown and poorly understood. During this new period, what once passed as absolute has become relativized: reason, history, the state, mankind. We express this by saying that those entities, those fetishes, have died. There is something true in this claim, but fetishes do not all die the same death. The death of "man" affects only our philosophers. The end of the state is always tragic, as is the end of morality and the family. Reflective thought allows itself to be captivated by these dramas and turns its gaze from the field before it, which remains blind. To explore this field, to see it, change is necessary, the abandonment of earlier viewpoints and perspectives. During this new period, *differences* are known and recognized, mastered, conceived, and signified. These mental and social, spatial and temporal differences, detached from nature, are resolved on a much higher plane, a plane of thought that can grasp all the elements. Urban thought (not urbanism), that is, the reflection of urban society, gathers the data that was established and separated by history. Its source, its origin, its stronghold, is no longer within the enterprise. It cannot prevent itself from assuming the point of view of the encounter, of simultaneity, of assembly, the specific features of *urban form.* In this way it rediscovers the community and the city, but at a higher level, on a different scale, and after their fragmentation (negation). It recovers the key concepts of a prior reality and restores them in an enlarged context: forms, functions, urban structures. It is constituted by a renewed space-time, a topology that is distinct from agrarian (cyclic and juxtaposing local particularities) and industrial (tending toward homogeneity, toward a rational and planned unity of constraints) space-time. Urban space-time, as soon as we stop defining it in terms of industrial rationality—its project of homogenization—appears as a *differential,* each place and each moment existing only within a whole, through the contrasts and oppositions that connect it to, and distinguish it from, other places and moments. This space-time is defined by *unitary* (global: constitutive of wholes, of groups formed around a *center,* of diverse and specific centralities) as well as *dualistic* properties. For example, the street can be considered an *incision-suture.* We should also learn to distinguish, without separating them, location and exchange, the transfer of information and the transport of material goods. To define these properties of urban differential space (time-space), we need to introduce new concepts, such as *isotopy, heterotopy,* and *utopia.* An isotopy is a place (topos) and everything that surrounds it (neighborhood, immediate environment),[2] that is, everything that makes a place the *same place*. If there is a homologous or analogous place somewhere else, it is part of that isotopy. However, alongside this "very place" there is a *different place,* an *other place*.

What is it that makes such a place different? Its *heterotopy:* a difference that marks it by situating it (situating itself) with respect to the initial place. This difference can extend from a highly marked contrast all the way to conflict, to the extent that the occupants of a place are taken into consideration. These places are relative to one another in the urban complex. This assumes the existence of a neutral element, which can consist of the incision-suture of juxtaposed places: street, square, intersection (intersection of streets and paths), garden, park. Now, there is also an elsewhere, the non-place that has no place and seeks a place of its own. Verticality, a height erected anywhere on a horizontal plane, can become the dimension of elsewhereness, a place characterized by the presence-absence: of the divine, of power, of the half-fictional half-real, of sublime thought. Similarly, subterranean depth is a reversed verticality. Obviously, the u-topic in this sense has nothing in common with an abstract imaginary. It is real. It is at the very heart of the real, the urban reality that can't exist without this ferment. Within urban space, elsewhere is everywhere and nowhere. It has been this way ever since there have been cities, and ever since, alongside objects and actions, there have been situations, especially those involving people (individuals and groups) associated with divinity, power, or the imaginary. This is a paradoxical space where paradox becomes the opposite of the everyday. *Monumentality* is diffused, radiates, becomes condensed, concentrated. A monument extends far beyond itself, beyond its facade (assuming it has one), its internal space. Height and depth are generally part of monumentality, the fullness of a space that overflows its material boundaries. In the cities of the ancient world, nothing escaped this monumentality because it was plural (plurality: sacred buildings, political buildings, palaces, theatricalized meeting places, stadiums, etc.). So what had no place to speak of—divinity, majesty, royalty, justice, liberty, thought—was at home everywhere. Not without contradictions, of course.

This urban space *is* concrete contradiction. The study of its logic and formal properties leads to a dialectical analysis of its contradictions. The urban center fills to saturation; it decays or explodes. From time to time, it reverses direction and surrounds itself with emptiness and scarcity. More often, it assumes and proposes the concentration of *everything* there is in the world, in nature, in the cosmos: the fruits of the earth, the products of industry, human works, objects and instruments, acts and situations, signs and symbols. These can be embodied anywhere. Anything can become a home, a place of convergence, a privileged site, to the extent that every urban space bears within it this possible-impossible, its own negation—to the extent that every urban space was, is, and will be concentrated and poly(multi)centric. The shape of the urban space evokes and provokes this process of concentration and dispersion: crowds, colossal accumulation, evacuation, sudden ejection. The urban is defined as the place where people walk around, find themselves standing before and inside piles of objects, experience the intertwining of the threads of their activities until they become unrecognizable, entangle situations in such a way that they engender unexpected situations. The definition of this space contains a null vector (virtually); the cancellation of distance haunts the occupants of urban space. It is their dream, their symbolized imaginary, represented in a multiplicity of ways—on maps, in the frenzy of encounters and meetings, in the enjoyment of speed "even in the city." This is utopia (real, concrete). The result is the transcendence of the closed and the open, the immediate and the mediate, near and far orders, within a *differential reality* in which these terms are no longer separated but become immanent differences. A thought that is moving toward concrete unity (selectively) reuses particularities that have been raised to the level of difference: local, regional, national, ethnic, linguistic, ethical, aesthetic. In spite of any efforts at homogenization through technology, in spite of the constitution of arbitrary isotopies, that is, separation and segregation, no urban place is identical to another. My analysis may seem somewhat formal. In fact, it applies to New York and Tokyo as much as it does to Paris. It is a way of illuminating an urban society, with its immanent dialectic, which extends past and future along a new plane. Perhaps, through this unitary and differential thought, we will enter a period that is no longer part of history, a time when particularities confronted one another, when uniformity struggled with heterogeneity. Gatherings, encounters, and meetings (although not without their specific conflicts) would supplant the struggle between separate and now antinomic elements. In this sense, it would be *posthistoric.*

Therefore, the urban considered as a field is not simply an empty space filled with objects. If there is blindness, it does not arise simply because we can't see these objects and the space appears empty. No, the urban is a highly complex field of tensions, a virtuality, a possible-impossible that attracts the accomplished, an ever-renewed and always demanding presence-absence. Blindness consists in the fact that we cannot see the shape of the urban, the vectors and tensions inherent in this field, its logic and dialectic movement, its immanent demands. We see only things, operations, objects (functional and/or signifying in a fully accomplished way). With respect to the urban, there is a twofold blindness, whose emptiness and virtuality are masked by plenitude. The fact that this plenitude is called urbanism only serves to more cruelly illuminate the blind. Moreover, this plenitude borrows the objects and products, the industrial operations and technologies of the previous epoch of industrialization. The urban is veiled; it flees thought, which blinds itself, and becomes fixated only on a clarity that is in retreat from the actual.

The (relative) discontinuities between the industrial and the urban are masked and misleadingly smoothed over (as they were and often still are between the rural and the industrial). If this blindness toward industry, its possibilities and demands, had not existed, would we have allowed it to invade the world, ravage nature, sow the planet with horror and ugliness throughout the course of a blood-soaked history? Would we have placed our limitless confidence in its rationality? Such considerations may seem utopian—and they are! And yet both Saint-Simon and, later, Marx believed, projected, that we could control and guide the process of industrialization. They weren't satisfied with understanding a blind process by leaving it in darkness or even simply illuminating it. Today, the urban reality itself, with its problematic and practice, is hidden, replaced by representations (ideological and institutional) that bear the name "urbanism." The name plugs the hole, fills the in-between. I'll return to this later.[3]

The confusion between the industrial (practice and theory, whether capitalist or socialist) and the urban ends up by subordinating one to the other in a hierarchy of actions, considering the urban as an effect, a result, or a means. This confusion has serious consequences, for it leads to the production of a pseudoconcept of the urban, namely, *urbanism,* the application of industrial rationality, and the evacuation of urban rationality.

The (difficult) transition is methodological and theoretical as much as, if not more than, it is empirical.

Every era has its own forms of authoritarianism, reformism, and revolution. We could also say that every period, every era, every sphere has its own forms of alienation and disalienation, which conflict in ways that are unique to themselves. In the first field, the agricultural sphere, historically the family and patriarchal society grow and flourish (and slavery can seem like a positive development). This is followed by the growing importance of family life and the social relations of feudalism (at least in Europe, where feudalism is established on a territorial basis, the seigneur being "eminent" master of a fief, the head of one or more villages). Since agrarian structures generally shift toward a concentration of property, history retains the signs of countless revolutionary movements: local or generalized revolts, jacqueries, brigandage, vigilante groups motivated by varying ideologies, frequently mystical. Finally, the concentration of property in the hands of allied or rival feudal lords, followed by a bourgeoisie that itself joined forces with or fought those feudal lords, resulted in *agrarian reform* projects. The widespread demand for land and the transfer of vast amounts of property provided the impetus for revolutionary movements that would transform the entire society: the French revolution of 1789, the Russian revolution of 1917, the Chinese and Cuban revolutions.

The period of industrialization gave rise to the well-known paternalism of the company owner or boss. At times, and even now, patriarchalism (peasant) and paternalism (industrial) became superimposed and strengthened one another, giving rise to an ideal head of state. Because industrialization makes considerable demands (capital accumulation, the use of all of a country's resources, a form of planned organization that extends corporate rationality to every aspect of a country's life), it has contradictory political consequences: revolution and authoritarianism, with both processes interacting in so-called socialist countries. These reforms and revolutions, the result of the process of industrialization, have become intertwined, a phenomenon that characterizes the period that has just ended.

The symptoms of the transition to the urban period are already beginning to manifest themselves. Urban paternalism is rampant, although masked by the figures of previous ages. The urban "notables" who exercise authority share in the prestige of the Father and the Captain of industry. Urban reform, which would clear the soil of the servitude that results from private property (and consequently from speculation), already has a revolutionary component. Entire continents are making the transition from earlier forms of revolutionary action to urban guerrilla warfare, to political objectives that affect urban life and organization (without being able to omit or resolve the problems of industrial and agricultural organization superimposed on this). The period of urban revolutions has begun.

This confirms the assumption of three successive fields throughout historical time. I should add that the most recent, the one that is currently emerging, acts simultaneously as a catalyst and analyst of the field, or rather of preexisting fields (agrarian and industrial). It focuses and precipitates characteristics that were vague and confused. It clarifies unresolved conflicts and contradictions by reactivating them (for example, in South America). Thus, the rise of industrialization, along with the new relations of production (capitalist), revealed the characteristics of peasant (and feudal) society, relations that were veiled within a turbid transparency for those who "lived" them without understanding them.

The hierarchy of this society (experienced as family and neighborhood relationships), the exploitation (experienced as a protective relation, as subordination of the community to the seigneur as "judge"), appeared for what they were. Similarly, today, the urban reveals the industrial, which appears as a hierarchy that is paired with a highly refined form of exploitation. Decision-making centers (urban) help us read these complex relationships in situ. They project them onto the soil, visibly contrasting the organizational activity of the "decision makers," supported by those who own and administer the means of production, with the passivity of the "subjects" who accept this domination. Moreover (although this is not the place to develop the idea fully), societies that did not experience a crisis during industrialization will undoubtedly do so during urbanization, since these two orders of causes or reasons can be superimposed, combined, or offset. Using these concepts, we can study the current situation in the United States, South America, nonsocialist Asia, and so on.

During this vast process of transformation, space reveals its true nature as (1) a political space, the site and object of various strategies, and (2) a projection of time, reacting against and enabling us to dominate time, and consequently to exploit it to death, as it does today—which presages the liberation of time-space.

is trying to present how studying the urban issued and used > other disciplines can't do it

> can't exist about utopie

3 || The Urban Phenomenon

analysing the urban phenomenon in the context of the REAL.

—importance of structures & limitations.

From this point on I will no longer refer to the city but to the urban. Having introduced the concept of the urban and its virtual nature in chapter 2, I would now like to analyze the phenomenon in the context of the "real" (the quotes around the world "real" reflect the fact that the possible is also part of the real and gives it a sense of direction, an orientation, a clear path to the horizon).

Today, the urban phenomenon astonishes us by its scale; its complexity surpasses the tools of our understanding and the instruments of practical activity. It serves as a constant reminder of the theory of *complexification,* according to which social phenomena acquire increasingly greater complexity. The theory originated in the so-called natural sciences and the general theory of information, but has shifted toward social reality and our understanding of it. Social relations have never been simple, even in archaic society. The Cartesian schema of primitive simplicity and the complication obtained by combining simple elements must be abandoned. The theory of complexification may seem to be philosophical and even idealistic (ideological), but is in fact based on

45

a number of scientific arguments. Every reality contains "elements" that can be revealed by analysis. These constitute its internal order (its consistency and coherence) but appear to us in a state of disorder that yields information within redundancy (repetition of order, of a preexistent grouping made up of discrete units or cataloged elements). For information brings with it an element of surprise and increasing variety, a disorder that arises from a new form of intelligibility, a new redundancy, a different and more complex momentary order.[1]

The urban phenomenon is based on descriptive methods, which are themselves varied. Ecology describes a "habitat," inhabited areas, neighborhood units, types of relations (primary within a neighborhood, secondary or derivative within an enlarged space). Phenomenological description, which is more subtle, investigates the links between city dwellers and a site; it studies the environment, the disparities of space, monuments, the movements and boundaries of urban life. Empirical description emphasizes morphology. It accurately measures what people see and do within an urban framework, a given city, a megalopolis (a dispersed city that forms an administrative and political whole, including urban functions, even when the older forms and structures have disappeared).

These methods reveal certain aspects, certain features of the urban phenomenon, primarily its enormity and complexity. But will they enable us to get closer to this phenomenon? After a certain point, description, no matter how detailed, turns out to be inadequate, and the limits of morphology and ecology are soon reached. Description is unable to explain certain *social relations*—apparently abstract with respect to the given and the "lived"— which appear concrete but are only immediate. These include relations of production and exchange and market relations (although we should really speak of markets). These relations are both legible and illegible, visible and invisible. They are projected onto the land-

[handwritten margin note: once "social relations" can be grasped — urban reality is clarified]

scape in various places: the marketplace, stock and commodities exchanges, labor exchanges, et cetera. Their projection enables us to identify those relations but not to grasp them. Once they are grasped at this level, the urban reality assumes a different appearance. It becomes the sum, the home of various markets: the market for agricultural products (local, regional, national), industrial products (received, manufactured, distributed on site or in the surrounding territory), capital, labor, lodging, land for development, as well as the market for works of art and the intellect, signs and symbols.

But it is not enough to define the urban by the single fact that it is a place of passage and exchange. The urban reality is not associated only with consumption, with "tertiary" activities, distribution networks. It intervenes in production and the relations of production. The constraints associated *[handwritten margin note: urban reality]* with description impede thought at this level. We elude the problematic, we avoid crucial questions such as those involving the center and centrality, and thereby risk promoting the decay of these centers or their development as elitist and authoritarian structures. In doing so we substitute ideology for description. In place of this, we should abandon phenomenology for analysis and logic for dialectics. To give you some idea of the analytical difficulties at this level, I'd like to refer to a study conducted by the Institute for Urban Sociology in France. The study attempted to break down the urban phenomenon into various factors, indicators, and indexes. It began with macro information (number of inhabitants per acre, age of the buildings, etc.) and gradually moved toward increasingly greater detail (fertility rates, education of qualified laborers, etc.). The number of indexes that were identified rose to 333. The analysis was stopped at this figure, arbitrarily, although an increasingly finer breakdown could have been attempted. After reducing the number to about 40 of the most typical indexes, the data set became difficult to manage, even on a computer. The urban phenomenon was presented as a global (or even a *total*) reality involving the entire range of social practices. Such globality can't be immediately comprehended. It is far more convenient to approach the global through a series of levels and stages—a difficult procedure, for with each step we risk running into various obstacles and mazes. With each faltering movement, with every advance, an ideological interpretation arises, and this is immediately changed into some form of *reductive and partial practice*. A good example of these totalizing ideologies (which reflect harmful practices) can be found in the representations of economic space and development that culminate in the elimination of a specific urban space through the absorption of social development into industrial growth, the subordination of urban reality to general planning. The politics of space sees space only as a homogeneous and empty medium, in which we house objects, people, machines, industrial facilities, flows, and networks. Such a representation is based on a logistics of restricted rationality and motivates a strategy that destroys the *differential spaces* of the urban and "habiting" by reducing them.

Every specialized science cuts from the global phenomenon a "field," or "domain," which it illuminates in its own way. There is no point in choosing between segmentation and illumination. Moreover, each individual science is further fragmented into specialized subdisciplines. Sociology is divided into political sociology, economic sociology, rural and urban sociology, and so forth. The fragmented and specialized sciences operate analytically; they are the result of an analysis and perform analyses of their own. In terms of the urban phenomenon considered as a whole, geography, demography, history, psychology, and sociology supply the results of an analytical procedure. Nor should we overlook the contributions of the biologist, doctor, or psychiatrist, or those of the novelist or poet. Geography studies the site of an agglomeration and its situation in a regional, national, or continental territory. Along with the geographer, the climatologist, geologist, the specialist in flora and fauna also supply key information. Demography studies populations, their origins, sex ratios, fertility rates, growth curves, and so on. What does the economist study, whether a specialist in urban reality or in general phenomena of growth? There is no shortage of objects: production and consumption within the urban context, income distribution, strata and classes, types of growth, the structure of the population (active or passive, secondary or tertiary). Historians are preoccupied with the genesis of a given agglomeration, the events and institutions that have affected its development. Without the progressive and regressive movements (in time and space) of analysis, without the multiple divisions and fragmentations, it would be impossible to conceive of a science of the urban phenomenon. But such fragments do not constitute knowledge.

Every discovery in the fragmentary sciences leads to a new analysis of the total phenomenon. Other aspects, or elements, of the totality appear, are revealed. It's not impossible that, starting with the theory of hierarchical interactions (homeostases), we could define certain urban realities by replacing the old organicism and its naive finality with more rational concepts. Starting with a formalized theory of graphs (trees and lattices), it wouldn't be impossible to elaborate models of urban space.[2] In terms of methodology, it has been recommended that we approach the urban phenomenon using the formal properties of space before studying the contradictions of space and its contents, that is, the dialectic method. Linguistics has recently made a number of advances, which have enabled it to identify the concept of a system of signs (and significations). Nothing prevents us from considering the urban phenomenon using this method or from this point of view. That the city and the urban phenomenon are rich (or poor) in signs, significations, and meanings is certainly not without interest. That the city and the urban phenomenon *system of signs / signification*

constitute a *system* (definable by signs that can be identified using a linguistic model, whether that of Jakobson, Hjelmslev, or Chomsky) has become dogma. The concept of a system of signs doesn't encompass the urban phenomenon, however. Although there may be a language of the city (or language in the city), or urban discourse and "writing," and therefore the possibility of semiological research, the city and the urban phenomenon can't be reduced either to a single system of signs (verbal or otherwise) or to a semiology.

Urban practice overflows these partial concepts and, consequently, theory. Among other things, this practice teaches us that we produce signs and significations that we sell and consume (for example, the advertising rhetoric of real estate). Also, it is unlikely that there is, in the city and within the urban phenomenon, a (unique) system of signs and significations; rather, there are several, on several levels. They include the modalities of daily life (objects and products, signs of exchange and use, the deployment of merchandise and the market, the signs and significations of *habiting* and "habitat"), of urban society as a whole (the semiology of power, strength, and culture considered as a whole or separately), of particularized urban space-time (the semiology of features characteristic of the city, its landscape and appearance, its inhabitants). If, within the urban space, there were only a single system of signs, associated with objects or acts, it would become dominant; we would never be able to escape its power. But how would we have entered it? Whatever the limitations of semiology applied to urban reality may be, it is still remarkable that recent developments in science reveal new aspects of that reality. From this point of view, our research has just begun. It poses problems that we are unable to separate from the "urban problematic" but nevertheless need to distinguish.

Let's consider for a moment the speech act, the event, from a conventional point of view. Ever since Saussure, we have analyzed discourse *(parole)* as a manifestation of language and language itself as a system. The actual manifestation (the event: I speak to someone) has as a precondition the existence of the system, its *virtual* existence. What makes communication possible—namely the act of communication as a succession of operations (encoding, decoding)—is a set of rules: phonological, morphological, grammatical, lexical, semantic. These rules enable us to construct, to produce, comprehensible arrays (sentences). Such an array is collective, whereas the act (the event) is individual. It has a coherent form (systematized, intelligible). However, this systematic array, which has been investigated over time from Saussure to Chomsky, controls the act (the event) without ever being completely manifested in it. Whether we are dealing with an ordinary succession of words or a subtle phrase, the system is the same. Speakers may employ it without realizing it, but they don't necessarily ignore it. The sentences produced have very different qualities (expressions, interdependence, relation to logical or practico-sensible referents). All speakers know their language. They have no need to deliberately specify the rules, and they use them as they see fit. A condition for the efficiency of this systematic array is the *absence* of system at the level of effects, acts, and events, even though its *presence* is manifest to varying degrees. In action the system operates within this *presence-absence*. Communication is possible only to the extent that the speaking "subject," the everyday speaker, remains blind with regard to that which determines and structures his discourse: the language system with its paradigms and syntactic structures. Once he begins to think about it, he enters a realm of metalanguage. And yet, it is not-being-blind that is responsible for the quality of the discourse. The system conceals itself from our awareness yet clarifies it more or less, for better or worse. This necessary concealment cannot be absolute, and understanding brings it out into the open. Incidentally, what is true for language is true for music. The effect, the impression or emotion, in no way implies a knowledge of the system's laws (harmony, composition).

Couldn't the urban be conceived along these lines? Couldn't it be considered a virtuality, a presence-absence? In this sense, linguistics could contribute to an analysis of the urban phenomenon. This is not to say that the urban is a language or sign system, but that it can be considered to be a whole and an order, in the sense given to those terms by linguistics.

It would be tempting to adopt this approach, connecting it with a theory of blind fields and differential analysis. But we should be on our guard and not overlook the limitations (as shown by earlier studies) of conceiving language as a system of *differential* elements (strictly determined and defined by their differences). Such a theory claims that all *signification* results from a process of differentiation, whose elements (discrete constitutive units) have a given signification through their oppositions or combinations but not in and of themselves (unless they are ready to enter this system of oppositions and combinations). In this sense, phonemes (sounds, which are assigned letters in Western languages) and signs are arbitrary. As are words. This creates a significant problem. Can such a theory, developed by Saussure and Trubetzkoy and their disciples, stand, given that meanings are constituted from *relations among already signifying units?*[3]

The Saussurian postulate presents us with a rule, according to which analysis is based on differences within the object, which we can intelligibly subdivide and reconstruct. Can this be done with units that are already signifying? Can we broach the distance (which has almost become "institutionalized") between the data of "lived experience," that is, the data of social practice, and the discourse used to articulate them? Between reality and its description or transcription? Possibly, to the extent that signifying elements are grouped into new oppositions and enter into clearly determined sequences. Is it the same for the urban, however? The urban groups elements from the countryside or from industry. Does it add to them or impose on them an order of some kind? Do known oppositions—center and periphery, open and closed, high and low—constitute urban paradigms or syntagms? Possibly. Only in-depth analysis can tell us whether the relation established between *distance* and *discourse* is valid or demonstrate the importance of such a formal structure and its limitations. Most likely we will have to refine our notion of difference, as developed by linguists, if we want to understand the urban as a *differential field* (time-space).

This complexity makes interdisciplinary cooperation essential. The urban phenomenon, taken as a whole, cannot be grasped by any specialized science. Even if we assume as a methodological principle that no science can turn its back on itself but that each specialization must maximize the use of its own resources to comprehend the global phenomenon, none of these sciences can claim to exhaust it. Or control it. Once we've acknowledged or established this, the difficulties begin. How many of us are unaware of the disappointments and setbacks that resulted from so-called inter- and multi-disciplinary efforts? The illusions of such studies, and the myths surrounding them, have been abundantly criticized. Participants at colloquia speak at cross-purposes and without any common ground among them; their main problem is one of terminology. In other words, language. Rarely do they agree on the words and terms they use, and even less rarely on the underlying concepts. Their assumptions and theories are for the most part incompatible. Confrontation and disagreement pass for success. Discussions skirt controversial topics. Assuming they actually succeed in identifying the "objects" of their discussion, they rarely follow the well-known rule of substituting the definiens for the definiendum without a breach of logic.

The methodological and theoretical difficulty increases once we take into account the fact that individual researchers are attempting to synthesize information. However, so-called interdisciplinary research remains open-ended, or rather exposed, empty, inconclusive. Frequently, it simply wraps itself around some artificial synthesis. While it is true that the urban phenomenon, as a global reality, is in urgent need of people who can pool fragmentary bits of knowledge, the achievement of such a goal is difficult or impossible. Specialists can only comprehend such a synthesis from the point of view of their own field, using their data, their terminology, their concepts and assumptions. They are dogmatic without realizing it, and the more competent they are, the more dogmatic. This gives rise periodically to a kind of scientific imperialism in fields such as economy, history, sociology, demography, and so on. Every scholar feels other "disciplines" are his auxiliaries, his vassals or servants. He oscillates between scientific hermeticism and confusion—academic Babel. During interdisciplinary conferences, it becomes impossible to maintain specificity without separation, or unity without mixture. Because participants have to stop at some point, because seminars and colloquia—as well as academic recognition—are not limitless, the result is usually some form of mediocre compromise. Convergence fades into the distance.

The urban phenomenon is *universal,* which would be sufficient justification for the creation of a university devoted to analytic research on the subject. In doing so, there is no need to insist on absolute priority over other kinds of research and disciplines that are already institutionalized—the humanities, arts, and sciences. What is needed is a department that can focus existing disciplines on an analysis of the urban phenomenon: mathematics (statistics, set theory, information theory, cybernetics), history, linguistics, psychology, sociology. This would require a change in our ideas about education, for such a discipline would be based not on a body of acquired knowledge (or what passes for such knowledge) that it can dispense but on a *problematic*. Paradoxically, at present a certain unity of knowledge can only be created around a coordinated set of problems. Acquired knowledge has begun to fragment; it crumbles in our hands, in spite of the pious efforts of epistemologists (who manage only to assemble the provisional results of the intellectual division of labor into little "balls" of knowledge). However, the status of such an institution—university or department—is not so clear. From the outside, such a project seems attractive, yet there are a number of obstacles to be overcome. For one, we risk duplicating, within an institution, the things that take place during intermittent exchanges among scholars. How can we manage to convince specialists that they need to overcome their own terminologies, their lexicons, their syntax, their way of thinking, their jargon, their professional slant, their tendency toward obscurantism, and their arrogance as owners of a domain? Imperialism remains commonplace. We see it today in linguistics and ethnology the way we once did with political economy. What can be done to deter specialists from trying to gain ascendancy for their discipline, which is to say, for themselves? We know from experience that anyone who is unable to maneuver with sufficient tactical skill is quickly reduced to silence and subservience. The project for creating a department of urbanism (or "urbanology" or "politology," dreadful neologisms) doesn't prevent us from yielding to the myth of interdisciplinary studies or the myth of some final synthesis. Research such as this can't work miracles. Creating such a department will not, in and of itself, ensure an exhaustive analysis of the urban phenomenon. Moreover, can there be such an analysis? Or of any reality for that matter?

The farther a given science pushes its analysis, the more it reveals the presence of a *residue*. It is this residue that evades its grasp. And, although essential, it can only be approached using different methods. The economist, for example, is faced with "something" that escapes him, which is, for him, this residue. Yet this evasive "something" is a part of psychology, history, and so on. More generally, numbers and measurement reveal dramas of which they are not a part. The specialist washes his hands of them. Although psychology, sociology, and history can draw attention to these dramas, they are unable to exhaust them or reduce them to some definite and final knowledge, to known and classified concepts. This would be true of social work, productive activity in industry, political rationality and irrationality. It would be truer still of the urban phenomenon—number and drama. The science of such a phenomenon could result only from the convergence of all the sciences.

However, if every discipline were to succeed in bringing into view some residue, they would all soon become irreducible. Their difference is reflected in this irreducibility, which calls into question the possibility of any form of convergence. Either we affirm the irreducibility of the urban phenomenon with respect to the fragmentary sciences taken together, as well as the science of "man" and of "society"—which is not without risk—or we identify mankind (in general), society (in general), or the urban phenomenon with the residual whole. This has theoretical interest but involves risks of a different sort: irrationality, for example. The problem remains: How can we make the transition from fragmentary knowledge to complete understanding? How can we define this need for *totality*?

We can also assume that the complexity of the urban phenomenon is not that of an "object." Can the concept of an object (of a science) withstand close examination? Apparently more precise and more rigorous than the concept of a "domain" or "field," it nonetheless brings with it significant complications. For the object presents itself, or is presented,

object

as *real* prior to any examination. It is said that there is no science without an object, no object without a science. Yet can we claim that political economy explores or possesses or constructs an isolatable object? Does sociology or history? Can we claim that urban economy has its own subject, or urban sociology, or the history of the city? Not as far as I am concerned. Especially since the "city" object exists only as a historical entity.

Nor is it reasonable to assume that our understanding of the urban phenomenon, or urban space, could consist in a collection of objects—economy, sociology, history, demography, psychology, or earth sciences, such as geology. The concept of a scientific object, although convenient and easy, is deliberately simplistic and may conceal another intention: a strategy of fragmentation designed to promote a unitary and synthetic, and therefore authoritarian, model. An object is isolating, even if conceived as a system of relations and even if those relations are connected to other systems. It is the intentionality of the system that is dissimulated beneath the apparently "objective" nature of the scientific object. The sought-for system constitutes its object by constituting itself. The constituted object then legitimates the system. What is disturbing about this is that the system under consideration may purport to be a *practice*. The concept of the city no longer corresponds to a social object. Sociologically it is a pseudoconcept. However, the city has a historical existence that is impossible to ignore. Small and midsize cities will be around for some time. An image or representation of the city can perpetuate itself, survive its conditions, inspire an ideology and urbanist projects. In other words, the "real" sociological "object" is an image and an ideology!

The urban reality today looks more like chaos and disorder—albeit one that conceals a hidden order—than an object. What is the scope or role of what is referred to as urbanism? There are a number of urbanists, some of whom are architects. If they are already familiar with the urban order, they have no need for a science. Their urbanism already contains this knowledge; they grasp the object and enclose it in its system of action. If they are unfamiliar with the urban order, whether hidden or being formed, they are in need of a new science. Then what exactly is urbanism? An ideology? An uncertain and incomplete practice that claims to be global? A system that implies the presence of technological elements and relies on authority to assert itself? A heavy, opaque body, an obstacle on a path, a false model? It is reasonable to ask such questions and to expect a clear, well-substantiated answer.

Rather than being an object that can be examined through contemplation, the reality of the urban phenomenon would be a *virtual object*. If there is a sociological concept, it is that of "urban society." And yet, such a concept is not limited to sociology. Urban society, with its own specific order and disorder, is in the process of formation. This reality envelops a whole range of problems: the urban problematic. But where does this phenomenon lead? Where is the process of urbanization leading social life? What new global or partial practices does it imply? How can we understand the process theoretically and provide practical guidance? Toward what? These are the kinds of questions urbanists face, and they have turned to specialists for the answers. But specialists have no answers, certainly no straightforward answers.

To become global, to overcome its inconsistency, social practice requires synthesis. Industrial practice, for example, has achieved a high degree of consistency and efficiency, mostly through planning and scheduling. Urban practice assumes it will follow this path. However, interdisciplinary research, which proceeds analytically, must avoid errors along the path to synthesis; more specifically, it must avoid extrapolation. Yet theoreticians and practitioners, conceptualizers and users demand synthesis. I must again insist that such synthesis cannot be the work of the sociologist, or the economist, or any other specialist, for that matter. Although, as practitioners, architects and urbanists claim to fulfill this role by avoiding the imperialism of specialization. Why? Because they can draw, because they possess certain skills, because they carry out plans and projects? Hardly. In fact, they succumb to the situation mentioned above. The imperialism of know-how, of drafting and the draftsman, is no better than that of the economist or demographer or sociologist. Knowledge cannot be equated with skill or technique. It is theoretical, provisional, changeable, disputable. Or it is nothing. However, there is "something" and someone. Knowledge escapes the "all or nothing" dilemma. The technocratic ambition of being able to synthesize from a given technique or partial practice (the circulation of traffic, for example, or merchandise, or information) falls apart as soon as it is formulated.

Should we feed all the data for a given problem to a computer? Why not? Because the machine only uses data based on questions that can be answered with a yes or a no. And the computer itself only responds to questions with a yes or a no. Moreover, can anyone claim that *all* the data have been assembled? Who is going to legitimate this use of totality? Who is going to demonstrate that the "language of the city," to the extent that it is a language, coincides with ALGOL, Syntol, or FORTRAN, the languages of machines, and that this translation is not a betrayal? Doesn't the machine risk becoming an instrument in the hands of pressure groups and politicians? Isn't it already a weapon for those in power and those who serve them?

We could use forecasting for our synthesis. But forecasting extrapolates from known facts and trends—an order that is already known. However, we know that the urban phenomenon is characterized today by a critical situation in which we are unable to identify with any degree of certainty either definite trends or an order. On what would we base such forecasts—that is, a set of investigations about the future—once we have identified the elements for our study? What would such an effort add to our previously formulated hypothesis, that of complete urbanization, a hypothesis that reflects the critical phase we are now entering? In what sense would a forecast be more precise and more concrete than the perspective that reveals the intersection of lines identified by the fragmentary sciences?

We know that this fragmentary (specialized) knowledge tends toward the global and that, in spite of its claims, it produces only partial practices, which also claim globality (for example, urban studies of highways and traffic). This fragmentary knowledge results from the *division of labor.* The division of labor in the theoretical domain (scientific and ideological) has the same functions and levels as it does in society. We need, however, to distinguish between the *technical division of labor,* rationally legitimated by the instruments and tools, by the organization of productive activity within the enterprise, and the *social division of labor,* which gives rise to unequal functions, privileges, and hierarchies, and which is related to class structure, the relations of production and ownership, institutions and ideologies. The technical division is modeled on the enterprise. The social division requires an intermediary that has become essential to it: the market and exchange value (commodities).

The division of labor in knowledge is transformed into institutions (scientific, cultural), together with their frameworks and devices, norms and values, and corresponding hierarchies. These institutions maintain their separateness and sow confusion. Thus, knowledge is based on distinct institutions and an entity, Culture. Created in and by the social division of labor, that is, in the market, these institutions serve it in turn, they adopt it by adapting it, as needed. They work literally for and in the social division of intellectual labor,

division of labor

which they dissimulate beneath the "objective" requirements of the technical division of labor, transforming the "technical" relations among sectors and domains, procedures and methods, concepts and theories into a hierarchy of prestige and income, administrative and managerial functions. This vast operation is based on divisions, which it reinforces by sanctioning them. Under such conditions, how can we achieve, or even hope to achieve, totality? The operation of such scientific and cultural institutions may extend beyond the satisfaction of immediate market needs and demands (for technicians, specialists, etc.), but their "creativity" can never escape the domain of the ideologies associated with this market. And what are these ideologies? Like institutions, they are *superstructures* that are elaborated or erected during a determinate period, namely industrialization, within equally determinate social frameworks (competitive capitalism, neocapitalism, socialism). At one time competitive capitalism tried to adapt to industrialization superstructures that were marked by a long period in which agricultural production and peasant life were dominant. More recently, neocapitalism has continued this effort, although it has been unable to contain the urbanization of society. Yet, by pushing illusion and appearance as far as they will go, a given institution will attempt to assume control of totality, while sanctioning divisions and reuniting them only within some Babelic confusion.

With respect to the approaching urban society, wouldn't this now be the role, the function of urbanism? Classical philosophy and traditional humanism thought they could achieve this by keeping their distance from the division of labor (technical and social) and the segmentation into fragmentary knowledge, as well as the inherent problems associated with this theoretical situation. Similarly, the university has for centuries claimed access to universality, in cooperation with classical philosophy and traditional humanism.

But it can no longer continue to fulfill this "function" to the extent that it institutionalizes the social division of labor, helping to organize, nurture, and accommodate it. Isn't this the function assigned to the university today? To adapt itself to the social division of productive labor, that is, to the increasingly stringent requirements of the market, the technical division of intellectual labor and knowledge? Science (like urban reality) has become a means of production and has become politicized in the process. Can a philosophy that arises from the separation of physical and intellectual labor, and is subsequently consolidated in spite of or even in opposition to this separation, still claim to be a totality?

This is a difficult situation. At one point it looked like abstract thought had successfully undergone the most trying ordeals; it appeared to have come back to life throughout the sciences after our "speculative Holy Friday" (Hegel) and the death of the Logos embodied in classical philosophy. Pentecost held even more surprises. The specialized intelligentsia received the gift of languages from the Holy Spirit, and linguistics assumed the role of the science of sciences, a role that had been abandoned by philosophy, which was supposed to have supplanted religion. Under cover of this false unity and confusion, which by no means excluded the existence of fragmentation and arbitrary segmentation, industrial practice imposed its limitations.

It is worth noting that *positivism* continues to present itself as a counterweight to classical philosophy, to its speculative developments. The positivist clings tightly to scientific facts and methodology. He sticks to the facts and treads lightly among concepts. He is suspicious of theory. There is a positivism of physics, biology, economics, and sociology, in other words, physicalism, biologism, historicism, economism, sociologism, and so on. Wouldn't there also be an urbanistic positivism, which accepts and confirms existing facts, which acknowledges them without asking questions, at times even pushing any form of questioning aside? And wouldn't this be related to technocratism? For positivist thought, it is irrelevant whether the findings from which it proceeds result from division or illumination, whether or not there is an "object" before it. Facts are classified and specified as being part of a given science or technology. However, positivism has never been able to prevent the leap from empiricism to mysticism or from linguistic precision to jargon (more or less esoteric). Moreover, this trend, according to which philosophy no longer has, or never had, meaning, is not incompatible with full-fledged imperialism. The specialist affirms the exclusive validity of science, sweeping aside other "disciplines" or reducing them to his own. This is how a logico-mathematical empiricism has tried to impose mathematical models on all the sciences, impugning the concepts specific to those sciences. Economism, for example, excludes any level of reality other than that associated with political economy and growth models. For several years now we have witnessed a growing enthusiasm for linguistic models, as if linguistics had acquired but a single definitive model, as if this model could be transplanted from its original environment to confer on other disciplines—psychology or sociology—a rigorous epistemological status. As if the science of words was the supreme science because everything is spoken and written with words!

In point of fact, the above interpretation finds fertile ground in philosophy; it is already (or still) philosophy, although not as classical philosophy understood it. Whenever positivism attempts to extend its properties (its own domain) and scope of activity, whenever it threatens or invades other territories, it moves from science to philosophy. It utilizes, consciously or not, the concept of totality. It abandons the fragmentary, the divisional, the analytic. As soon as we insist on synthesis and totality, we extend classical philosophy by detaching its concepts (totality, synthesis) from the contexts and philosophical architectures in which they arose and took shape. The same is true for the concepts of system, order, disorder, reality and possibility (virtuality), object and subject, determinism and freedom, structure and function, form and content. Transformed by scientific knowledge, can these concepts be separated entirely from their philosophical development? At this point we enter the realm of metaphilosophy.

Philosophy has always aimed at totality. But whenever philosophy has tried to achieve or realize totality using its own resources, it has failed. And it failed because it lost its way among speculative abstractions. Yet it is philosophy that supplies this scope and vision. And it is from philosophy that other fields have borrowed the concept of totality whenever they extrapolate from some form of acquired knowledge that they believe to be final and from which they attempt to draw some kind of universal rule. The philosopher and philosophy can do nothing by themselves, but what can we do without them? Shouldn't we make use of the entire realm of philosophy, along with scientific understanding, in our approach to the urban phenomenon? So we can examine its processes, its trajectory, its horizon, and especially, when considering "humankind's being," its realization or failure in the coming urban society? Nothing prevents philosophy and its history from assuming a different form as project (but whose?) while on this trajectory. Philosophy already assumed this guise when illuminated by industry and an emergent industrial practice. What prevents it from assuming the meaning it had in connection with the city and the town, *metaphilosophy* separating from philosophy the way urban society emerged from the dispersed city? This meditation won't take place outside philosophy or inside philosophy, but beyond philosophy, as a specialized, constituted, and instituted activity—the very definition of metaphilosophy.

Because it is situated beyond philosophy, metaphilosophy frees itself of the institutional discourse associated with philosophy as an institution (academic, cultural). Philosophy since Hegel has become institutionalized; it is a public service in the service of the state, and its discourse can only be ideological. Metaphilosophy does away with this servitude. What exactly does this enigmatic word imply (a word that corresponds to Aristotelian metaphysics, although on a completely different level)? That thought takes into account concepts that have been elaborated by philosophy as a whole (from Plato to Hegel) and not concepts specific to a given philosophy or system? And just what are these general concepts? We can identify and enumerate them: theory and practice, system and totality, element and set, alienation and disalienation.

The goal is not to reconstruct a faded humanism, which has been compromised ever since Marx and Nietzsche subjected it to their scathing theoretical criticism. But how can we know if urban society will enable the development of a new humanism, so-called industrial society, capitalist or not, having effectively rejected its earlier forms? There is always the possibility that such an investigation of philosophy, brought about through the intermediary of metaphilosophy, may end in failure. The urban problematic cannot reject such a possibility out of hand without falling back into the old idealist categories of faith and defiance.

What could philosophy provide? Initially, a form of radical critique. Then, a radical critique of the fragmentary sciences as such. This approach would reject any form of dogmatism, including that of totality or its absence, the efforts of the fragmentary sciences and their pretension to comprehend and clarify everything, as well as the withdrawal of the individual sciences to a well-defined object, sector, field, domain, or system considered as private property. In this way radical critique can define a methodological and theoretical *relativism*, an epistemological pluralism, which affects objects (including the corpus constituted for and by a given specific field of research, and therefore including the urban phenomenon considered as a corpus) as well as models, which are always provisional. No method can ensure absolute "scientificity," whether theoretical or practical, especially in sociology (whether urban or not). Even mathematics and linguistics are unable to guarantee a perfectly and definitively rigorous methodology. Although there are models, none of them can be realized completely satisfactorily, none of them can be generalized, or transferred, or exported, or imported outside the sector within which they were constructed without exercising considerable precaution. The methodology of models is said to continue and refine the methodology of concepts. There are specific concepts, characteristic of each partial science, but none of them can completely determine an object by tracing its contours, by grasping it. The effective realization of an object involves considerable risk; even if the analyst constructs objects, these are provisional and reductive. Consequently, there are many models that do not constitute a coherent and completed whole.

The construction of models in general, and specific models in particular, is not devoid of criticism. A model is worthwhile only if we use it, and using it consists in measuring the difference between models, and between each model and the real. Rather than constructing models, critical reflection provides an orientation, which opens pathways and reveals a horizon. That is what I am proposing here: not so much to construct a model of the urban as to open a pathway toward it. Science, or rather the sciences, move forward the way we build roads or conquer lands by sea. How could there exist a scientific "corpus" (corpus scientiarum), a single definitively established "body" or unchangeable core? Constructing such a corpus would mean confusing experimental and theoretical, empirical and conceptual research and, in consequence, verifiable and therefore falsifiable *hypotheses*,[4] which are revisable and always contain an ideological component once they have been formalized and axiomatized. What appears to have been established through demonstration is transformed, appears (or will appear) under a different guise, including the axioms and forms that thought has isolated in all their purity. Sooner or later radical critique reveals the presence of an ideology in every model and possibly in "scientificity" itself.

Today, the philosophical approach can be used to destroy *finalism*. Originating in philosophy, and more specifically in metaphysics, traditional finalism collapses in the face of the onslaught of criticism. In terms of historical becoming, and given the inevitability of change, there is no definite, prefabricated goal, one that is therefore already achieved by a god or in his name, by an Idea or absolute Spirit. There is no objective that can be posited as an object (already real). Conversely, there is no preexisting impossibility associated with a planned goal, for an objective that is rationally claimed to be the meaning of action and becoming. No synthesis can be accomplished in advance. There is no original and final totality compared with which any relative situation or act or moment would be alienated-alienating. On the other hand, there is nothing to contradict the exigency, the will, and the idea of the total, nothing to enclose the horizon, except this alienating-alienated attitude, which declares the exclusive existence, theoretical and practical, of a *thing*. The urban (urban society) is not a prefabricated goal or the meaning of a history that is moving toward it, a history that is itself prefabricated (by whom?) to realize this goal. Urban society provides a goal and meaning for industrialization only to the extent that it is engendered by it, encompasses it, and directs it toward some *other thing*. It is no longer a metaphysical conception, naively historical, of finality. So from whom and from what can totality emerge? From a strategy and a project that extend ancient philosophy along a new

plane. Thus, the philosopher (or rather the metaphiloso-
pher) no longer claims to provide finality, synthesis, totality.
He challenges the philosophy of history and society just as he
challenged classical metaphysics and ontology. He intervenes
to remind us of the demands of totality, that is, the impossibility of accepting fragmentation and confirming separation. He provides a radical critique of finalism in general as
well as the particular finalisms of economism, sociologism,
and historicism. Once it has become metaphilosophy, philosophy no longer reveals an already accomplished or lost
reality: "mankind." It points toward a path, an orientation.
But although it may supply conceptual instruments to cut
a path to that horizon, it is no longer the terrain through
which the march of time occurs. It reveals the extent of the
problematic and its immanent contradictions, especially the
relation between a self-affirming, self-developing, and self-
transforming rationality and an old, collapsing finality. Yet
rationality seemed to imply finalism and in effect did imply
it in its speculative conceptions of the universe. If rationality
is supposed to evolve from speculation to global rational
practice, from political rationality to social rationality, from
industrial rationality to urban rationality, it can only do so
by resolving this immanent contradiction. The goal? The
end? They are conceived, projected, and declared but can
only succeed if they are able to accommodate the most com-
prehensive strategy possible.

Current discussions of humankind, the human, and humanism duplicate the arguments used by Marx and Nietzsche
against classical philosophy and its implications. The criteria put forward during these arguments, that of a rational
coherence, which would be substituted for harmony and
"human scale," clearly correspond to a need. Today's society
is in such a state of chaos that it cries out for coherence. However, whether or not coherence alone is sufficient has yet
to be demonstrated. The path that has been opened leads

toward the reconstruction of some form of humanism in, by, and for urban society. Theory is cutting a path toward this emerging "human being," toward fact and value. This "being" has needs. An analytic of need is required. This does not mean that a philosophy of need based on Marxism, sociology, psychology, or industrial rationality can be developed. Quite the contrary. Instead of a "positive" study of needs designed to establish and classify them, such knowledge could be constituted through the analysis of errors and inadequacies in architectural practice and urban ideology. Wouldn't an indirect and negative method be more pertinent than sociological positivism? If there are "functionalizable" needs, there is also desire, or there are desires, that straddle the needs inscribed in things and language. Moreover, needs are only retained, received, and classified on the basis of economic imperatives, of social norms and "values." The classification and the denomination of needs thus have a contingent character and are, paradoxically, institutions. Institutions are created on top of such needs, controlling and classifying while structuring them. Prior to those needs is situated, global yet indistinct, a "something" that is not a thing: impulse, élan, will, desire, vital energy, drive. Why not articulate these differences in terms of "id," "ego," and social "superego," the id being desire, the superego institution, and the ego a compromise? What prevents us from doing so? Still, we run the risk of falling back into the philosophy of need and the ontology of desire. Pointlessly.

Looking at this more in terms of our own day-to-day experience and speech, we can say that the human being starts life as a child, then enters adolescence, followed by adulthood. Prematurity and immaturity tend toward maturity, and life's end. Maturity arrests our human development, is our death warrant. The dialectical anthropology now being developed, which is based on a consideration of the urban (habiting), would find its point of departure and biological support in the theory of fetalization.[5] The progeny of egg-laying species are left to fend for themselves. Once the eggs are hatched, usually in large numbers, the young that emerge nearly fully formed are left on their own. The waste is enormous. Fetalization protects the young, but once they are born, they are unable to take care of themselves. This leads to a long period of infancy and adolescence, when the offspring are simultaneously incomplete, weak, and educable—"plastic," in other words. This misery has a counterpart in educability, but even here there are problems. Sexual maturity doesn't follow overall maturity, whether psychological or social, but precedes it. This can result in disturbances (which have been investigated by psychoanalysis). The human group comprises both incomplete beings, some of whom have infinite possibilities (indeterminate), and mature, or complete, beings. How can we constitute a form, *habiting,* which would help this group to live? This—here anthropologically formulated—is the question posed by habiting (architecture). The concept deliberately rejects philosophical finalism, that of a human ascension free from disruptive contradictions, a preestablished harmony, which is still found today in the self-satisfied worldviews supplied by official Marxism, the followers of Teilhard de Chardin, and humanist theology. We know that the slow maturation of the human being, which results in its dependence on the family, on housing and on "habiting," on the neighborhood and the urban phenomenon, implies educability and, consequently, an astonishing degree of plasticity. This being, whose growth and development are out of sync, possesses both urgent and deferred needs. There is something in this being that makes it identical to its predecessors, analogous to its peers, and yet different. Its grandeur results from its misery; its lack of harmony and dysfunctionality propel it forward, toward its end. It never casts off this ambiguity. The dramatic and conflictual character of needs and desires has an anthropological

fundamental needs.

element. This still uncertain science can only be constituted dialectically, by taking contradiction into consideration. The human being has a "need" to accumulate and forget, as well as a need, whether simultaneous or successive, for security and adventure, sociability and solitude, satisfaction and dissatisfaction, disequilibrium and equilibrium, discovery and creation, work and play, speech and silence. Home, dwelling, lodging, apartment, neighborhood, quarter, city, and agglomeration have responded, continue to respond, or no longer respond to some of these needs. Theories about a family "environment," a work "environment," a "functional framework" or "spatial framework," supplied to meet these needs, are nothing but dogmatic monstrosities, which run the risk of creating monsters from the human larvae that are supplied to them.

The current (social and urban) reality reveals a number of fundamental needs, not directly but through that which repressively controls, filters, overwhelms, and distorts them. Those needs are discovered only belatedly. We know the past from the present, not the present from the past, thus legitimating a historicity without historicism. Marx indicated the theory and the process clearly in his work. A dialectical anthropology could be developed from an urban problematic. In turn this knowledge would provide data for the problematic and for the solution to related problems. But it couldn't claim to formulate or resolve all those problems by itself. Such knowledge is an element of the disciplines involved and possesses no special status of its own, other than to have come into existence along with the problematic in question.

An anthropology of this nature brings together elements or aspects of ancient philosophy. What can it learn from them? That there is a kind of "human material," which, although governed by laws (biological, physiological), assumes *no preexisting form* within so-called social or human reality. However, it is endowed with extraordinary plasticity and a

presence-absence

remarkable sense of educability and adaptability. Forms appear, conceived and willed, capable of modeling this material according to various postulates and possibilities. These forms act at different levels. Within the limits of the possible, doesn't urban society also present us with a new form?

Even the most die-hard specialists don't disdain the use of rationality. Can they be ignorant of the fact that the concept of rationality is inconceivable without philosophy, even and especially if philosophical reason is only a moment or an element of rationality? By claiming that rationality is free of context, absolute, we mutilate it and render it unyielding. This is an important point and not without controversy (see the diagram that follows). Over the years, reason has assumed a succession of different forms. The logical reason formulated by Greek thought (Aristotle) was followed by analytic (Descartes and European philosophy) and dialectical reason (Hegel and Marx, contemporary research). Each form served as a critique of its predecessors but did not destroy them, which led to new problems. Similarly, the philosophical reason developed by Western tradition was followed by *industrial practical reason* (Saint-Simon, Marx, etc.), which has been supplanted more recently by the emerging *urban rationality*. In a social rather than mental context, the rationality of *opinion* has given way to the rationality of *organization,* which must incorporate questions of finality and meaning associated with the rationality of *fulfillment*. With respect to that finality and meaning, abstract humanism (liberal and classical) has been able to maintain its ideological presence only by being subjected to the examination of critical humanism. This in turn gave rise to a fully developed (therefore tending toward totality), concrete humanism. The first stage of humanism corresponds to the image of the human being, an abstract project presented and represented by philosophy. The second stage corresponds to the awareness of the existence of a goal, a meaning. During the third stage, the concept of and will to plenitude (finished, relative, but "total") was developed.

Reason and rationality

logic	philosophical	opinion
analytic	industrial	organization
dialectic	urban	fulfillment

Humanism

abstract humanism	image and project
critical humanism	challenge
developed humanism	finality (project)

Space (social, urban, economic, epistemological) is unable to provide form, meaning, or finality. However, it is common to see space presented as a rule, a norm, or a superior form, which has found consensus among intellectuals and even developed into a "corpus" for the sciences. Yet space is only a medium, environment and means, an instrument and intermediary. It is more or less appropriate, that is to say favorable. It never possesses existence "in itself" but always refers to something else, to existential and simultaneously essential time, subjective and objective, fact and value—because it is a supreme "good" for the living, whether they live well or badly; because it is simultaneously end and means. But this has nothing to do with philosophy or intellectuals—physicists, biologists, historians, sociologists. The articulation of "time-space," or, if you prefer, the inscription of "time in space," becomes an object of knowledge. Is this an object in the commonly understood sense, one that is isolatable, an object with a definite contour? Certainly not. Is it a sociological object then? Possibly, but only negatively, something felt to be inadequate. The relation between time and space that confers absolute priority to space is in fact a social relationship inherent in a society in which a certain form of rationality governing duration predominates. This reduces, and can even destroy, temporality. Ideology and science are merged. The relation becomes part of an upside-down world that also needs to be "stood on its feet."

I'd like to return to those fragmentary sciences for a moment. How should we think of them? There are several hypotheses about how we should go about this:

1. *Convergence.* Convergence is the hope and myth expressed at interdisciplinary conferences. It is assumed that we can define convergence on familiar terrain, as if it were a highway intersection. But this intersection can't be defined and can never be reached. If convergence exists, it exists on the horizon, in perspective. But we still need to determine how to "put things into perspective." In the here and now, our orientation is not toward traditional "mankind" but toward the reconsidered and reconstructed "human being" of an emerging urban society.

2. *Integration* (of fragments defined by fragmentary disciplines). But with what? With some intellectual discipline that has been made dominant? This is unacceptable. With a praxis? But here the concept of praxis would collapse in the face of radical critique. If it isn't class strategy, it is merely a recourse, a postponement. And a likely failure made more likely by certain worrisome precedents such as the failure of economism, an ideology and practice based on a fragmented conception of the world.

3. *Pragmatism.* This is the use of information supplied here and there by someone or other (a sociologist, for example). This happens often. Scientificity turns into its opposite—the lack of rigorous criteria.

4. *Operationalism.* This is a variant of pragmatism. It is accompanied by an ideology of technocracy and bureaucracy, along with its attendant myths. Only operational concepts are sought. The validity of concepts is no longer demonstrated. We limit ourselves to demanding that they

possess the ability to classify, that is, some *administrative* capacity. Sometimes we push them farther. Operator and manipulator act in concert.

5. *Hierarchization.* Who is going to establish valuations? Who is going to claim that sociology is worth more than geography or demography? Norms will become the norms of institutions and their rivalries, the last traces of free competition. Intellectuals will give politicians the keys to the city of science. They will decide; they will declare what is normal and what is not, which will result in a general state of anomie (the abnormal, the pathological), depending on their intentions and representations. Here the (methodological) concept of *level* can be used to bolster our argument. But if each specialist occupies a level in a hierarchy, questions of priority and precedence become essential. Which is, at the very least, inconvenient.

6. *Experimentalism.* Analysts provisionally dissect "abstract" objects; they study with the help of different descriptions, temporarily considered auxiliaries. They then compare them against experiments (testing) in the field. This is a feasible approach, but one in which we abandon totality and with it the objective (if not the object), and thus the goal and its meaning as well. With totality we lose finality and the coherence and rationality we have been looking for. We risk vacillating between abstract utopianism and short-term realism, between irrationality and utilitarianism. We also run the risk of handing over to others (and they are not even worth identifying by name) the power to make decisions.

None of these options is satisfactory, rationally speaking. However, they do reveal something: it is impossible to bring specialists (in the fragmentary sciences) together around a table on which we place an "object" to be understood or constructed. The most competent among them are the least reliable. It is impossible to assume that such a meeting could even take place. Impossible to summarize such specialized, dispersed knowledge, analyses couched in divergent vocabularies, based on "points of view" that are already disjunct, particularized, and limited.

What is to be done? I would like to put forth again the concept of an *urban strategy*. This implies making distinctions between political and social practice, between day-to-day and revolutionary practice, in other words, between *structure* and *praxis*. Social practice can be analyzed as *industrial practice* and *urban practice*. The first objective of this strategy would be to strip social practice from industrial practice and orient it toward urban practice, so that the latter can overcome the obstacles barring its path.

habiting & habitat

4 || Levels and Dimensions

— used to analyse the urban phenomenon

geographic economic sociological etc readings of the urban.

In analyzing the urban phenomenon, we can make use of the common methodological concepts of dimensions and levels. These concepts enable us to introduce a degree of order into the confused discourse about the city and the urban, which mixes text and context, levels and dimensions. Such concepts can help to establish distinct codes, either juxtaposed or superimposed, for decrypting the message (the urban phenomenon considered as message). They serve as lexical items (readings) in urban texts and writing, or maps, and as "urban things," which can be felt, seen, and read in the environment. Does this mean there are geographic, economic, sociological (etc.) readings of the urban text? Most likely. Obviously, ordering facts by means of these concepts does not exclude other forms of discourse, other classifications, other readings, other sequences (geopolitical, organizational and administrative, technological). Earlier I briefly discussed the problem of convergence, at least provisionally.

Diachronically, on the space-time axis, I indicated (without insisting on any absolute divisions) the levels reached by emerging economic and social structures or, as is so often said, using a somewhat vague term, by "society." In short, the rural, industrial, and urban succeed one another. I would now like to construct a synchronic picture of this latter term. Looking at present-day society, I distinguish a *global* level, which I'll indicate with the letter *G;* a *mixed* level, which I'll indicate with the letter *M;* and a *private* level, *P,* the level of habiting.

Power—the state as will and representation—is exercised at the global level. As will, the power of the state and the people who hold this power are associated with a political strategy or strategies. As representation, politicians have an ideologically justified political conception of space (or no conception, which leaves the field open for others to promote their particular images of time and space). At this level, these strategies are accompanied by various *logics,* which—although with some reservations—we can refer to as "class logics," since they generally consist of a strategy that is pushed to its ultimate conclusions. Along similar lines, we can also speak of a "socio-logic" and an "ideo-logic." Political power makes use of instruments (ideological and scientific). It has the capacity for action and is capable of modifying the distribution of resources, income, and the "value" created by productive labor (surplus value). We know that in capitalist countries today, two principle strategies are in use: *neoliberalism* (which maximizes the amount of initiative allowed to private enterprise and, with respect to urbanism, to developers and bankers) and *neo-dirigisme,* with its emphasis (at least superficially) on planning, which, in the urban domain, promotes the intervention of specialists and technocrats, and state capitalism. None of these strategies is airtight, however. Neoliberalism leaves a certain amount of space for the "public sector" and activities by government services. Neo-dirigisme cautiously encroaches on the "private sector." Moreover, diversified sectors and strategies can coexist: there can be a tendency toward centralized planning or even socialization in agriculture, liberalism in housing, (limited) planning in industry, circumspect control of the movement of capital, and so on. The global level accommodates the most general, and therefore the most abstract, although essential, relations, such as capital markets and the politics of space. This makes it more responsive to the practico-sensible and the immediate. Simultaneously social (political) and mental (logical and strategic), this global level projects itself into part of the built domain: buildings, monuments, large-scale urban projects, new towns. It also projects itself into the unbuilt domain: roads and highways, the general organization of traffic and transport, the urban fabric and neutral spaces, "nature preserves," sites. It is the level associated with what I refer to as *institutional space* (along with its corollary, institutional urbanism). This assumes, if not a system or systems of explicit action, at least some form of systematized action (or "concerted" actions that are conducted systematically). The very possibility of such logics, of such unitary systems, at the state level demonstrates that the old "town-country" distinction is in the process of disappearing. This does not mean that it is outmoded. And one has to ask whether the state, which claims to have undertaken this mission, is really capable of carrying it out. The *social* division of labor, in which the market (for products, capital, and labor itself) is implicit, no longer seems to function spontaneously. It requires the control of a superior organizational power, the state. Conversely, this power, this supreme institution, tends to perpetuate its own conditions, to maintain the separation of manual and intellectual labor, as it does the separation between the governed and the governing, and possibly between town and country. Doesn't this then introduce new contradictions into the structure of the state? As will, it transcends the separation of town and country. This would lead it to strengthen decision-making centers, changing the urban core into a citadel of power. And doesn't it also, simultaneously,

represent urbanization and overall development as being de-
centralized, dividing the country into zones, some of which
will be singled out for stagnation, deterioration, and a return
to "nature"? The state could then be said to be organizing a
process of unequal development in an effort toward global
homogeneity.

Level M (mixed, mediator, or intermediary) is the specifically urban level. It's the level of the "city," as the term
is currently used. Let's assume we can mentally withdraw
(remove) from the map of the city (large enough for this
abstraction to have meaning) whatever is part of the global
level, the state, and society—namely buildings such as min-
istries, prefectures, and cathedrals—and whatever depends
on level P—privately owned buildings. Remaining on the
map will be a built and an unbuilt domain: streets, squares,
avenues, public buildings such as city halls, parish churches,
schools, and so on. After withdrawing any global elements,
we have intellectually removed whatever is directly associated with institutions and higher-level entities. What remains before us assumes a form that holds some relationship
to the site (the immediate surroundings) and the situation
(distant surroundings, global conditions). This specifically
urban ensemble provides the characteristic unity of the social
"real," or group: forms-functions-structures. In our case we
can speak of dual-purpose functions (*in* the city and *of* the
city: urban functions compared with the surrounding territory and internal functions) as well as dual-purpose structures (for example, for services such as trade and transport,
some of which operate in the "service" of the surrounding
area—villages, market towns, smaller cities—and others in
the service of urban life strictly speaking).

Level P appears (wrongly) to be somewhat more modest, even unimportant. Here only the built domain in the
form of various buildings is of interest: housing primarily,
including large apartment buildings, private homes both
large and small, campgrounds, shantytowns. Although the

distinction between "habiting" and "habitat" is already subject to considerable controversy, I still insist that it is useful.
"Habitat" denotes a concept or rather a caricatural pseudoconcept. Toward the end of the nineteenth century, urban
thought (if it can be characterized as such), strongly and
unconsciously reductive, pushed the term "habiting" aside,
literally enclosed it within parentheses. It opted instead for
"habitat," a simplified function, which limited the "human
being" to a handful of basic acts: eating, sleeping, and re-
producing. These elementary functional acts can't even be
said to be animal. Animality is much more complex in its
spontaneity. Level P can't be understood by opposing the
"microsocial," or molecular, with the "macrosocial," typical of
large aggregates or large structures. It isn't only the locus of
minor economic or sociological "agents," such as the family,
neighbors, and "primary" relations (the terms employed by
ecologists and the Chicago school). Habitat, as ideology and
practice, repulsed or buried habiting in the unconscious. Before habitat became commonplace, habiting was an age-old
practice, poorly expressed, poorly articulated linguistically or
conceptually, seen sometimes as vital and sometimes as degraded, but always concrete, that is, simultaneously functional, multifunctional, and transfunctional. During the reign of
habitat, habiting disappeared from thought and deteriorated
strongly in practice. It required the metaphilosophical medi-
tations of Nietzsche and Heidegger to restore the meaning of
the term. Habitat, ideology and practice, had even repressed
the elementary characteristics of urban life, as noted by a
very shortsighted ecology. These included the diversity of
ways of living, urban types, patterns, cultural models, and
values associated with the modalities and modulations of
everyday life. Habitat was imposed from above as the application of a homogeneous global and quantitative space, a requirement that "lived experience" allow itself to be enclosed
in boxes, cages, or "dwelling machines."

Although we cannot arbitrarily assimilate habiting to

the unconscious of psychology and psychoanalysis, there is a definite analogy—to the extent that our failure to recognize habiting can serve as an illustration of the theory of the unconscious. In order to rediscover the word and its meaning, in order even to utter them, we need to make use of concepts and categories that fall within the scope of the inhabitant's "lived experience," in proximity to the unknown and the misunderstood in the everyday, and go beyond, to general theory, to philosophy and metaphilosophy. Heidegger cleared the way to a restoration of the term when he commented on the forgotten (or misunderstood) words spoken by Hölderlin: "Poetically man dwells . . ." This means that the relation of the "human being" to nature and its own nature, to "being" and its own being, is situated in habiting, is realized and read there. Even though this "poetic" critique of "habitat" and industrial space may appear to be a right-wing critique, nostalgic and atavistic, it nonetheless introduced the problematic of space. The human being cannot build and dwell, that is to say, possess a dwelling in which he lives, without also possessing something more (or less) than himself: his relation to the possible and the imaginary. Philosophy tried to locate this relation beyond or within the "real," the visible and legible. It thought it had found it in transcendence or immanence, both of which were hidden. But if this relation is hidden, it is obviously so. One glance and the veil falls away. This relation resides in the dwelling and in habiting, in temples and palaces, the woodcutter's hut and the shepherd's cabin. A home and language are two complementary aspects of the "human being," as are discourse and urban realities, together with their differences and relations, whether hidden or evident. The "human being" (and not "mankind") cannot do anything but inhabit as poet. If we do not provide him with (as an offering and a gift) the possibility of inhabiting poetically or of inventing a poetry, he will create it as best he can. Even the most derisive

everyday existence retains a trace of grandeur and spontaneous poetry, except perhaps when it is nothing more than a
form of advertising or the embodiment of a world of commodities, exchange having abolished use or overdetermined
it. Concerning this poetry of habiting, we have a great deal to
learn from the East—China and Japan. Japanese homes have
a corner, the tokonoma, that contains a single object chosen
in harmony with the season (the weather). This object can
be simple or precious, a flower or piece of porcelain. Objects,
whether in good or bad taste, and which may or may not
saturate the space we inhabit, which may or may not form
a system, including the most atrocious bric-a-brac (kitsch),
are the derisive poetry men and women make use of to remain poets. Nonetheless, never has the relationship of the
"human being" with the world, or with "nature" and its own
nature (with desire, with its own body), experienced such
profound misery as during the reign of habitat and so-called
"urbanistic" rationality.

> Was bedeuten diese Haüser? Wahrlich, keine grosse Seele
> stellte sie hin, sich zum Gleichnisse. Nahm wohl ein blödes
> Kind sie aus seiner Spielschachtel? . . . Und diese Stuben und
> Kammern? Können Männer da aus—und eingehen?

> What do these houses mean? Verily, no great soul put them
> up as its likeness! Might an idiotic child have taken them
> out of his toy box? . . . And these rooms and chambers—can
> *men* go in and out of them?[1]

We have already seen that there is a relationship between
the "human being," understood analytically, and the form
that is given to it and that it receives by habiting. With respect
to this human being, the formal knowledge accumulated by
philosophy tells us that there is a contradiction between desire and reason, spontaneity and rationality. Anthropology,

with the support of other partial forms of knowledge, such as psychology and sociology, tells us that there are different ages and sexes. The simplicity of these statements is only apparent. The coexistence of ages, which is necessary if there is to be a group or a collective subject (family, neighborhood, friendships), is no less essential for the concrete (social) perception of time. This time has nothing in common with what we read on our wall clocks and wristwatches. It is a time of peril, of finitude, which fills every instant with gravity and makes every moment precious. The newborn child is not a tabula rasa, but is somehow still formless. It can only tend toward form, toward maturity, which marks an endpoint (in every sense of the word: finality, meaning, accomplishment, perfection, term, termination, conclusion). Maturity is fulfillment and already death. There is no reason for adults to behave proudly since they have already reached their end. Childhood, adolescence, and young adulthood, which are deficient in reality, clumsy, pretentious, even stupid (see Gombrowitz, for example), are incomparably rich with the greatest and most deceptive form of wealth: possibility. How can we create a habiting that gives form without impoverishing, a shell that enables the young to grow without premature closure? How can we provide a "home" for this ambiguous "human being" whose only escape from ambiguity is old age, who is ill-formed but magnificent, filled with contradiction, but in such a way that no single aspect of that contradiction can vanquish another without serious mutilation, a contradictory situation from which this "being" must nevertheless somehow escape? These problems already assume a subversive intellect that overturns our "model" of the adult, destroys the myth of paternity, and dethrones maturity as an "end." This, once correctly presented by uniting scientific knowledge and metaphilosophical meditation, is the problematic of habiting. This level is no less complex than the others because it is "minimal." A very remarkable and very strange ideology, based on Cartesianism and a de-generate form of analytic thought, identifies smallness with simplicity, size with complexity. Habiting should no longer be approached as a residue, as a trace or result of so-called superior levels. It should, it can already, be considered as a source or foundation, as essential functionality and trans-functionality. Theoretically and practically, we are reversing the situation, inverting meaning: what appeared to be sub-ordinate is now dominant. The predominance of the global, of the logical and strategic, is still part of the "right-side-up world" that we need to overturn. What I would like to at-tempt here is a reverse decoding of the habitual situation, but taking habiting rather than the *monumental* (this being not so much condemned as reconsidered) as the point of depar-ture. The dialectical and conflicted movement between habi-tat and habiting, simultaneously theoretical and practical, moves into the foreground. Semiology can play a role here, whether we use it to better understand the nonverbal signs and symbols scattered inside and outside our "dwellings" or the terms and syntagms used in the speech—monologues or dialogues—of architects and urbanists.

Critical analysis, however, need not be limited to semi-ology and linguistic methodology. The use of other concepts is inevitable, and it would be shortsighted to overlook the re-lationship (which appears to be misunderstood rather than simply unknown) between Eros and Logos, desire and space, sexuality and society. While it is true that during the indus-trial period the "reality principal" overwhelmed the "pleasure principle," hasn't the moment for its revenge arrived within urban society? Isn't sexuality a form of the "extrasocial so-cial"? Social because it is modeled, fashioned, cultivated, and alienated by society. Extrasocial because desire, tending toward anomie, assumes the mantle of mystery, strangeness, secrecy, even crime, to escape social norms and forms. Love, conjugal or otherwise, seeks "intimacy." More intense, more impassioned because suffused with guilt, because it knows it is being hunted, it acquires sociality and sociability only to spite society. How can we express, architecturally and urbanistically, this situation of a "human being" both incomplete and filled with contradictory virtualities? At the highest level, the socio-logic level, "objects" constitute a system. Every object communicates to every action its system of signification, which it acquires from the world of commodities, for which it serves as a vehicle. Every object contaminates every action. However, these systems do not have the characteristics of plenitude and completion implied by the assumption of a logic of space or things, for there are faults, voids, and lacunae everywhere. There are conflicts as well, including those between logics and strategies. The logic of space subjected to the limitations of growth, the logic of urbanism, of political space, and housing clash and sometimes break apart when they come into contact. The same is true for the logic of things (objects) and the logic of play (or sports). Social logics are located at different levels; there are cracks and crevices between them. Desire insinuates itself through these fissures. Without it "human material," being shapeless, would soon be forced into an absolute form, warranted and inspected by a state that is solidly resting on a mass of "subjects" and "objects." Without it everydayness would become hopelessly uniform. Even subversion would become unthinkable.

Along with the breakdown into various levels, we can also introduce the following:

1. The dimensions of the urban phenomenon. This refers not to the size but to the essential properties of the phenomenon:

   a. Social relationships have a surface area. This includes the most abstract relationships, those arising from commodities and the market, contracts or quasi contracts among "agents" on a global scale. The urban phenomenon and urban space, seen from this point of view, can be considered "concrete abstractions." Earlier, I pointed out how this dimension harbors a multiplicity of these abstractions (various juxtaposed, superimposed, and sometimes conflicting markets for products, capital, labor, works of art, and symbols, housing and land).

b. The urban phenomenon and urban space are not only a projection of social relationships but also a terrain on which various strategies clash. They are in no sense goals or objectives, but means and instruments of action. This includes anything specifically associated with level M, namely, institutions, organizations, and urban "agents" (important people, local leaders).

c. The urban phenomenon and urban space retain a reality and vitality that are specific to them. That is, there is an urban practice concerning space and its organization that cannot be reduced to global ideologies or institutions or to specifically "urbanistic" activities, which serve as means to often unknown ends.

2. Distinctions and differences concerning the *topological* properties of urban space, properties that theoretically constitute a network or system of pertinent oppositions (paradigm):

   a. the private and the public
   b. the high and the low
   c. the open and the closed
   d. the symmetric and asymmetric
   e. the dominated and the residual, et cetera.

This is an example of the well-known form of analysis by dimension, notably the *symbolic* dimension, which generally refers to monuments and, consequently, to ideologies and institutions, present or past: the *paradigmatic,* a set or system of oppositions, and the *syntagmatic,* a sequence (or path).

Starting with the breakdown into levels, it is possible, after introducing the pertinent oppositions, to construct a grid of urban space. To each level we assign an index of appropriate topological properties. For example, anything associated with the global (G) and public level, which is generally associated with height (h+), comprises mostly open spaces and other, tightly enclosed, spaces (0–), places of power or divinity, or both combined. This space, the space of grandeur, is sometimes marked by imposing symmetries (s+) and sometimes gives "free" play to asymmetric elements (s–).[2]

This is about as much detail as I want to provide here for this spatial grid. It is a subject that would be more appropriate in a work devoted not to the urban phenomenon in general, but to the analytics and politics of space, to urban topology. Also, it would risk masking the contributions and point of view of the present analysis as well as its position. Essence, foundation, and meaning are supplied by *habiting,* not by the other levels. Yet, in considering the grid on its own, all the levels appear to be governed by some general coherence, by a logic of space. This point of view can't be explicated without an immediate *critique.*

As can be seen from the above, these levels have *relative* importance. For politicians, the government level is obviously the most important, since it is where decisions are made, at least bureaucratic ones. This group has a strong tendency, we could say a tendency backed by force, to conceive of the other levels and dimensions of the phenomenon in terms of their formal knowledge (representation) and power (will). It is at this level that industrial practice, that of the enterprise, becomes ideology (representation) and will (reductive). The state and politicians are therefore reductive by their very nature and frequently on the offensive. This is further exacerbated by the fact that during the critical phase, these levels and dimensions tend to blur. The city explodes. The urban arrives. Complete urbanization is soon under way and yet, old-line bureaucracies (institutions and ideologies associated with earlier forms, functions, and structures) defend themselves, adapt to new situations.

The second level (M) appears to be essential. But to assume this would imply actively defending urban reality on the theoretical level. Yet this level is nothing but an intermediary (mixed) between society, the state, global power and knowledge, institutions, and ideologies on the one hand and habiting on the other. Wherever the global attempts to govern the local, whenever generality attempts to absorb particularities, the middle level (mixed, M) comes into play: it is a terrain suitable for defense or attack, for struggle. But it remains a means. It can never be an end, except temporarily and on behalf of a strategy that must at some point throw down its cards and reveal its hand. Can it protect existing urban institutions? Possibly. Can it promote them? Can it develop criteria and models? Can it extend to urban society (virtual and possible) the institutions and ideologies drawn from the city (of the past)? No. That would be impossible. Although urban reform might proceed in this manner, a more profound, more radical thought, one that grabbed things by their roots and was therefore more revolutionary, would affirm the durable primacy of habiting.

The two critical phases that intersect the urban in historical time can be defined as follows. During the first phase, the long dominant agrarian (agricultural production, rural life, peasant society) becomes subordinate to an urban reality initially propelled and soon ravaged by commerce and industry. There is a second reversal, a second inversion of meaning: a dominant industry becomes subordinate to urban reality. However, within this inversion a process of subversion is under way: a level that was always considered unimportant now becomes essential, namely habiting. At this point it can no longer be considered an effect, result, or accident with respect to the specific level of the urban, less so with respect to the global, which remains dependent on the industrial period (of productivist ideology, of political space subject to the requirements of growth). The urban is defined by the unity of these latter levels, with the last, or P level, predominating. This inversion of meaning is conceived and projected during the critical phase, increasing the sense of confusion. Aiming for something doesn't mean we will achieve it. This confusion also promotes hostile activities, the extent of which I'll discuss later. Here, I assume that the urban is primary and priority is given to habiting. This priority requires freedom of invention and the establishment of heretofore unknown relationships between urbanist and architect, with the final word being given to architecture. Architecture itself responds to a vague social request, which has never succeeded in becoming a social order. The subversion (theoretically) consists in the following proposition: the implicit request will become an explicit order.

Until now these social "orders" arose from industrial growth, that is, the ideologies and institutions established at level G, the state level. In other words, the urbanist submits to the requirements of industrialization in spite of his reticence and awareness of, or desire for, something else. As for the architect, he condenses (in the sense in which the term is used by Soviet architects between 1920 and 1925, the architect as "social condenser") existing social relationships.[3] Whether he wants to or not, the architect builds on the basis of financial constraints (salaries and payments) and norms and values, that is to say, class criteria that result in segregation even when the intention is to bring about integration and interaction. More generally, the architect is caught in the "world of commodities" without realizing that it is in fact a world. Unconsciously, that is, in good conscience, he subordinates use to exchange and use values to exchange values. Social orders are imperious, and the only request that is made is a direct or indirect expression of that order. If it aspires to something else, the request, being vague, is repressed. This is not a reason to abandon older cities and the virtual urban in the face of the attacks to which they are subject. On the contrary. Even if level M is defined only as a *mediator* (mixed) and not as something essential or central, it is still the site and nexus of struggle.

These statements may appear paradoxical. But there are untold numbers of unspoken paradoxes, and we do not create those we report, just as the person who warns us of a catastrophe or upheaval is not responsible for its occurrence. Some people, whether disingenuous or genuinely naive, blame meteorologists for the arrival of storms. During the process of general urbanization and the extension of urban territory, there was an attempt to liquidate urban reality. Wasn't this paradoxical? An empty challenge? The reflection of an ideology? Most likely. Yet this ideology drove a number of projects, or rather, was hidden behind projects with very different motivations.

These attacks against the "city" are not new. I would like to briefly summarize the arguments of its adversaries. As early as 1925, Soviet theoreticians criticized the large city, the metropolis before it came to be known as a *megalopolis*. They saw the metropolis as the creator of capitalism, a result of the maneuvering of the bourgeoisie to better control the working class. Although not false, the truth of this analysis is relative and short-lived. They demonstrated, not without subtlety, the defects inherent in the metropolis. Their argument was frequently used by others, even in the United States. The large city, monstrous and tentacular, is always political. It serves as the most favorable environment for the formation of authoritarian power. It is characterized by organization and overorganization. Large cities legitimize inequality. Faced with a choice between an overbearing sense of order and the everlasting threat of chaos, power, any power, state power, will always choose order. The large city has but a single problem: number. A mass society is established within its circumference, which implies that these masses be constrained and implies, therefore, the existence of a permanent state of violence and repression. What about the insurmountable opposition between "city and country," whose interactions have become catastrophic? The countryside knows it serves the city, but the city poisons nature; it devours it by recreating it in imagination so that the illusion of activity endures. Urban order contains and dissimulates a fundamental disorder. The large city is nothing but vice, pollution, and disease (mental, moral, social). Urban alienation contains and perpetuates all other forms of alienation. In it, through it, segregation becomes commonplace: by class, by neighborhood, by profession, by age, by ethnicity, by sex. Crowds and loneliness. Space becomes increasingly rare—it is expensive, a luxury and privilege maintained and kept up through a practice (the "center") and various strategies. The city does indeed grow richer. It attracts wealth and monopolizes culture just as it concentrates power. But it collapses under the weight of its wealth. The more it concentrates the necessities of life, the more unlivable it becomes. The notion that happiness is possible in the city, that life there is more intense, pleasure is enhanced, and leisure time more abundant is mystification and myth. If there is a connection between social relationships and space, between places and human groups, we must, if we are to establish cohesion, radically modify the structures of space. Moreover, is there a structure to urban space? Isn't the large city just a chaotic jumble once it is no longer segregation and separation? The concepts that seem to designate places and the qualities of space in fact refer only to social relationships embedded within an indifferent space: neighborhood, environment, and so on.

Pushing this analysis further, we can say that only the village, or parish, had a social and spatial structure that enabled a human group to appropriate its conditions of existence (environment, occupied places, the organization of time). It's true that these harmonious (social) bodies, or what passed as such, were also dependent on a strict hierarchy, an equilibrium between castes. Space alone was entirely filled with meaning, completely *signifying,* and it openly declared to one and all (that is, to each member of a caste, class, age, or sex) what was permitted and what was not. The physical place stipulated the role. The equilibrium of the community required virtues, respect, submission, and custom perceived as an absolute. All of this disappeared in the large city.

village

Although they stopped short of fetishizing the community (tribe, village, parish) or the "non-city," some Soviet theoreticians, around 1925, formulated the problem of the *optimum,* an issue that has been discussed interminably since then. How can we determine, how can we quantify (in terms of surface area, number of inhabitants) the urban optimum? What criteria can we use? Attempts to do so have always raised serious objections. Assume that the desirable optimum, because it can be administered (within what bureaucratic framework?), is fixed at roughly three hundred thousand inhabitants. Rarely would a city of this size be able to maintain a large university, a large theater, an opera, well-equipped and therefore expensive hospital services.

Recent projects have been implemented in which French highways would become streets in a future megalopolis, while maintaining both the relations between neighborhoods and a certain centrality (crossings and intersections) as well as wilderness areas and "virgin" spaces, distinct from industrial zones. Which demonstrates that all thought in this domain is utopian! Projects such as these anticipate the process of generalized urbanization. But if this is the case, what authorizes us to bring urban space and rural space together by building an urban society along our old highways? What motivates this movement backward, which, although it doesn't coincide with the shift toward a communitarian ideology (encouraged by ethnology), isn't necessarily distinct from it, either?

Arguments against the "urban" and in favor of the "non-city," and the corresponding principles, have more to do with morality than any connection between the real and the possible. The problems have been poorly expressed. Without trying to rekindle the controversy, I would like to point out that general urbanization and the extension of the urban fabric are already beyond their grasp. From now on society must confront problems of an entirely different order: either urban chaos or urban society conceived as such. More concretely, the attack on the (ancient) city and the (virtual) urban, whether or not they are intentionally confused, is being conducted on two levels: an upper level, G, and a lower level, P.

The attack from above, if we can call it that, includes a global project to subject the national territory to a process of "development" controlled by industrialization. There are two requirements here, and two postulates: space must be planned, and the particularities of sites and situations must acquiesce to more general constraints that are technologically motivated. At this point, *mobility* becomes essential for a population subject to changing constraints, determined by cataloged sets of variables, energy sources, raw materials, and so forth. Residential mobility, always fairly limited, will be resolved through increasingly greater professional mobility. (For example, because of labor costs and investment needs, the metallurgical industry in Lorraine shifted to Dunkirk, a port where minerals arrive from Mauritania; the town of Mourenx will disappear or be converted once its natural gas resources are exhausted.) From this point of view it is unacceptable that "sources of labor" will remain unexploited simply because they are attached to the land, are immobilized beneath layers of history, have become enracinated, and so forth. Such harsh truths apply globally, anywhere that economic, financial, or technological pressures disrupt structures (local, regional, or national) that vainly attempt to resist.

At the P level, motivations (considerably different) converge with technological and technocratic concerns. The enthusiasm for the ephemeral and nomadic, the fascination with incessant departures, will supplant the earlier sense of rootedness in the home, the traditional attachment to the place of birth. What do human beings want? Shelter. No matter where it is. Yona Friedman has built portable structures and units (boxes) that can be joined together to create one or more rooms of different sizes, ephemeral groupings.[4] From this perspective, we could generalize and democratize the luxury life of millionaires, who move from home to home, villa to villa, or yacht to yacht. Which exposes them to the pleasures of the world. Or so it seems.

Whether from above or from below, this would be the end of both habiting and the urban as sites of bundled opposition, as centers. This end of the urban would be brought about by the establishment of *industrial organization* as a system of acts and decisions—the end of *historical value* with respect to values and the *transformation of everyday life* with respect to cultural patterns or models.

Resistance to these two sources of pressure comes from both reactionary and revolutionary forces, and they need to be distinguished. In other words, criticism can come either from the "right" or the "left." The same holds true for any critique of the critique. The critique of the city on behalf of the older community (tribal, village, parish) is a critique from the right; the critique of the city (and the non-city), which I have undertaken here, is a critique from the left. Conventional attitudes and a more or less folkloric parochialism and regionalism protest the disappearance of the city. Protest based on *particularities,* generally of peasant origin, should not be confused with an opposition to repressive bodies or with an awareness and acknowledgment of *difference.* The affirmation of difference can include (selectively, that is, during a critical check of their coherence and authenticity) ethnic, linguistic, local, and regional particularities, but on another level, one where differences are perceived and conceived as such; that is, through their relations and no longer in isolation, as particularities. Inevitably, conflicts will arise between differences and particularities, just as there are conflicts between current interests and possibilities. Nonetheless, the urban can be defined as a place where differences know one another and, through their mutual recognition, test one another, and in this way are strengthened or weakened. Attacks against the urban coldly and lightheartedly anticipate the disappearance of differences, which are often identified or confused with folkloric particularities. Industrial ideology, whether technocratic or individualistic, is homogenizing.

It will be difficult for the defenders of the emerging urban society to avoid all ambiguity, to clear a path that leads straight to a goal. Take the question of the center and centrality, for example. There can be no city or urban reality without a center. Moreover, urban space is defined by the null vector. It is a space in which every point can virtually attract to itself *everything* that populates the surroundings—things, works, people. At every point, the time-space vector, the distance between content and container, can become zero. Although this is *impossible* (u-topian), it characterizes the dialectical movement (the immanent contradiction) of urban space-time. Therefore, it is theoretically impossible not to support urban concentration, together with the attendant risks of saturation and disorder, and the opportunities for encounters, information, and convergence. To attack or destroy it implies a form of empiricism that begins with the destruction of thought. The center can only be dispersed into partial and moving centralities (polycentrality) whose concrete relations are determined circumstantially. This being the case, we risk supporting decision-making and power structures, those that involve massive concentrations, enormous densities, of wealth and power. This means there can be no sites for leisure, festivals, knowledge, oral or scriptural transmission, invention, or creation without centrality. But as long as certain relationships of production and ownership remain unchanged, centrality will be subjected to those who use these relationships and benefit from them. At best it will be "elitist," at worst controlled by the military or police. Can we do anything other than accept the ambiguity and contradictions—that is, the dialectical nature of the situation and its processes? Accepting the situation does not mean supporting the dictatorship of centers of power and authoritarian planning. Far from it. Or rather, quite the contrary.

One point worth noting is that the social and professional mobility so desired by planners (primarily urban planners and moving companies) is fundamentally superficial. It does not refer to the intense mobility that can only occur near a center, but to the displacement of populations or materials that leave social relationships intact. Needless to say, such mobility can result in chaos. However, there is an even greater risk that it will end in "equilibrium" or "stability," since the displacement of people and their activities is highly programmed and "structured." This is not the disorder characteristic of information or encounters, but of boredom and neurosis. Within this a contradiction appears, which an intellectual strain known as "urbanism" attempts to resolve: order and disorder, equilibrium and movement, stability and mobility. To succeed it must tighten any existing constraints by imposing homogeneity, a *politics of space,* a form of rigorous planning that suppresses symbols, information, and play. Urbanists fail when they propose temporary constructions that endure: a monotonous morphology, a kind of stasis for people passing through because they want to go somewhere else to find something else. In this sense the urbanist and architect blend together. The architect thinks he is an urbanist, or vice versa. However, both of them, whether together or in opposition, receive orders and obey a single uniform social order. Moreover, they soon abandon the small grain of utopia, the slight touch of madness that might still distinguish their work and render them suspect of ill will, disobedience, or nonconformity. The politics of space implies a strategy that aligns levels and dimensions. Order cloaks itself in morality and scientificity. The dictatorship of the right angle merges with that of industrialization and the neocapitalist state. Gropius followed a similar orientation when he conceived of a "logical and systematic coordination in the treatment of architectural problems," when, during the founding of the Bauhaus, he anticipated a "total" architectonic that could be transmitted through "coherent, operational, and systematized" training.

What of that residential nomadism that invokes the splendors of the ephemeral? It merely represents an extreme form, utopian in its own way, of individualism. The ephemeral would be reduced to switching boxes (inhabiting). To suggest, as Friedman does, that we can be liberated through nomadism, through the presence of a habitat in the pure state, created with metal supports and corrugated steel (a giant erector set), is ridiculous. If at some time in the near future, the ephemeral becomes more prevalent, which is entirely conceivable, what would it consist of? In the activities of groups that are themselves ephemeral, that would invent and realize various works. Their own. In which their lives and their group existence would be realized and exhausted by momentarily freeing themselves of the everyday. But what works, what groups? The answer would render the fundamental question of creation irrelevant. Those groups, should they come into being, would invent their moments and their actions, their spaces and times, their works. And they would do so at the level of habiting or by starting out from that level (without remaining there; that is, by modeling an appropriate urban space). The few attempts in this direction, the few attempts to break through the system or systems of things and make the impossible possible, demonstrate nothing either by their failures or their successes. Such attempts would only be significant during the course of a revolutionary reversal of the upside-down world. They are and will be the work of what are referred to as "leftist" groups, whose designs existing society will attempt to co-opt. Unless, that is, the movement is able to win over society and push it in another direction. What about architectural initiatives? Or those of urbanists? It would be naive to think, as Hans Meyer did in 1928, when he replaced Gropius as the director of the Bauhaus, that "building means organizing social, psychological, technical, and economic life."[5] Architecture's demiurgic role is part of urban mythology and ideology, which are difficult to distinguish. Gropius, moreover, saw things in broad terms, suggesting that the architect serve as a coordinator who would unify problems, proceeding from "a functional study of the house to that of the street, from the street to the city, and finally to regional and national planning." Unfortunately, the opposite took place: structural planning subjected lower degrees and levels to its own constraints. Can this situation be reversed? The possible, associated with socially transformative activities, is currently impossible. It is not the architect who will "define a new approach to life" or enable the individual to develop himself or herself on a higher level by throwing off the weight of the everyday, as Gropius believed. It is the new approach to life that will enable the work of the architect, who will continue to serve as a "social condenser," no longer for capitalist social relationships and the orders that "reflect" them, but for shifting and newly constituted relationships. The architect may even be able to function as a "social accelerator," but the economic context that would make this possible must be examined carefully so we are not fooled by words or appearances.

Based on the above, we can redraw the space-time diagram as follows:

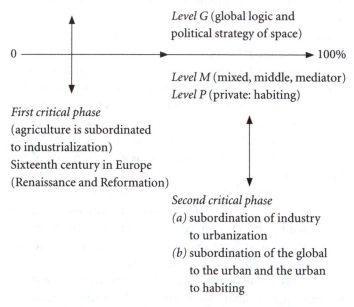

Level G (global logic and political strategy of space)

0 ————————————————→ 100%

Level M (mixed, middle, mediator)
Level P (private: habiting)

First critical phase
(agriculture is subordinated
to industrialization)
Sixteenth century in Europe
(Renaissance and Reformation)

Second critical phase
(*a*) subordination of industry
    to urbanization
(*b*) subordination of the global
    to the urban and the urban
    to habiting

A twofold reversal takes place here. The subordination of urban reality to its antecedents and conditions is overcome, as is the subjection of habiting to so-called higher levels of social practice. This results in a *fundamental* (in the sense of a bottom and foundation) reorganization.

An especially audacious, albeit very simple, interpretation of Marxist thought views Marx's work (*Capital* primarily but also his philosophical and political works) as an exposé of the world turned upside down and the attempt to right it; that is, to get it back on its feet. It is not only Hegelian philosophy and dialectic that has its head in the sand, its feet in the air and that finds itself discomfited (alienated) by a situation that custom has attenuated and made to appear normal. According to Marx, the world upside-down is a society with the following characteristics:

1. The intermediary replaces the producer (worker) and creator (artist, inventor, producer of knowledge and ideas) when he can enrich himself at their expense by capturing the results of their activities, leaving those who assumed the risk of creation in poverty. Who are these intermediaries? They are merchants and the many others who succeed in branching out into the circuit that runs from production to consumption and back again. In the immediate foreground would be the capitalist, whether rentier or active.

2. The state, which should serve all of society and extend its capacity for organization and rationality within it, manages to achieve the exact opposite. It strengthens the exploitation of society as a whole, it sets itself above society and claims to be the essential element of social life, its *structure*, whereas it is merely an accident (a *superstructure*).

3. Bureaucracy can develop its own interests and the means to serve them, where competence and formal knowledge become the means of selection for bureaucracy.

4. Effects appear as causes, and the end becomes the means and the means the end.

I have added a few elements to the theory of the upside-down world that strengthen the mission to reverse this world and complete the Marxist ideal of a revolution in the system of industrial organization with the addition of a planned urban revolution. It isn't hard to demonstrate that any other interpretation of Marxist thought is merely an interpretation, a weakened version, intended to address a given aspect of the upside-down world or a given institution: the state, philosophy, the division of labor, an existing morphology, and so on. It is just as easy to show that without such complet subversion, including the subversion that foregrounds problems about the actual locations where social relationships are conducted, whatever is being said about those relationships is nothing more than ideological discourse. It has been said many times, in keeping with Marx, that the "essence" of "man" cannot be found in the isolated individual but consists of a set of relationships or concrete (practical) social relationships. Generic Man (in general) is only an abstraction. What can we use as a reference to discern the traits of an individual? For a long time, this reference was biological. We borrowed it from the theory of Pavlovian reflexes, from the physiology of the brain. The cortico-visceral defined the individual. This reference was also, and still is today, most often technological (and therefore economic). It is in relation to productive labor that we can conceptualize and determine the constitutive relationships of consciousness (of personal life), assuming we are not talking into a void and we make an effort to reach a praxis of some sort. Would anyone deny that the references to industrial practice or biology are relevant? References to desire and the "unconscious" are as well, providing we don't fetishize this unconscious by substantializing it.

But can we examine such questions—about consciousness, about the development of the individual (within the group he or she is closest to or within groups in which he or she participates, from the family to globality)—without taking into account the morphology and forms offered by *places*, or the relationship between those places and institutions (school, university, business, army, state, etc.)? Such speculations persist, embodied within heady abstractions, covered by a mask or veil of philosophy.[6] The introduction of topology (analytic considerations of topoi in the mental and social space) can help us remain focused on the philosophical scope of these conceptions while eliminating any traces of philosophizing, that is, speculative, attitudes.

Nature vs urban

5 || Urban Myths and Ideologies

defines my ths of agrarian age — they respond to the questions & problems of a peasant society

There is little doubt as to the existence of agrarian myths or their ideological extension. Although the myths of the agrarian age are not necessarily agrarian myths, they incorporate elements (themes, signifying units) borrowed either from nomadic and pastoral life or nonagricultural productive activity (hunting, fishing, artisanship). There are no specific dates attached to the use of these myths. Here I define the myths of the agrarian age not by the agricultural nature of their themes, figures, and characters but by the fact that they respond to the questions and problems of a peasant society (predominantly agricultural, even if it comprises political cities). When Fourier imagined the emancipation of the community and a new model for the division of labor, one that was not based on agricultural labor (where everyone took turns assuming responsibility for all the tasks to be done), he was referring to an industrial myth that made use of agricultural elements, not an agrarian myth. A myth such as this is so close to an ideology that it is difficult to separate them. At the same time, the Fourierist utopia prepared and anticipated the most powerful affirmation of the industrial

103

epoch, which was taken over by Marx and made the core of revolutionary thought: the transcendence of a fragmented division of labor. There are two aspects to the analysis of a myth: the search for the elements of the myth and the determination of their reuse in another context. The elements can come from a period other than the one in which they are reunited, reused, or reworked. This, rather than the analysis, can be used to date the myth.

Can the myth of Atlantis in Plato's *Critias* be considered an urban myth, or an anticipation or presentiment of such? The myth reveals the contemporaneity, the nonpacific coexistence, of town and country from the very beginnings of Western civilization. Agricultural production and the peasants' relationship with nature give rise only to a cyclical image of time, which has no sense (direction), or rather, no other sense (interpretation) than that of the Great Year and the Eternal Return. As the image of a time that advances toward a final outcome or a cosmos that is harmoniously arranged within a luminous space, the City imposes its mark on thought. Atlantis, the magnificent, harmonious city, merges with the territory that it organizes and dominates. Doesn't Plato's mythic tale contain the Greek image of the Oriental city, the European echo of an "Asiatic mode of production"? However, in Greece, the political city is forcefully present and barely differs from the Oriental city. Around it are assembled peasant groups, villages, and producers (synoecism). It was an Eden in an ocean of fields, forests, jungles, and deserts, a land devoid of oppression or exploitation. It introduced a sense of harmony within the reciprocal tension of elements, like Heraclitus's lyre and the arch. It was like the memory of a lost continent, where the separation of life and work had no meaning, no place. Plato retained the myth and gave it form, which is to say that philosophic thought (which is based on the division and separation of activities, precisely when it struggles against them to restore a totality) addressed the problem of the ancient City and its rational, although threatened, institutions (the Logos that speaks and acts).

Conversely, the City provides philosophical reflection with re-presentations of its political existence—that of a center—within the immense rural environment. What do these reflections supply? What prophecy? What impossible-possible future? A kind of urban communism that would not be rural, or ascetic, or artisanal, but specific to the City, although not dependent on existing institutions associated with the City. It would be a utopia inherent in urban thought, through which the mythic text transcends its context, a utopia that had successors: the City of God, the City of the Sun. Utopian communism had urban as well as agrarian sources. If we had to classify and date the myth of Atlantis, we would classify it among the urban myths. But wouldn't the *Critias* be unclassifiable as a philosophical narrative, a mixed form of discourse consisting of myth, ideology, and utopia? Myth could be defined as a *noninstitutional discourse* (not subject to the constraints of laws and institutions), whose elements are taken from the context. Ideology would consist in an institutional discourse justifying and legitimizing (or criticizing, refusing, and refuting) existing institutions but unfolding through them. Utopia would transcend the institutional by making use of myth, the problematic of the real and the possible-impossible. Needless to say, noninstitutional discourse cannot occur just anywhere, or be uttered by just anyone. It arises from a specified, if not specialist, group with anomic tendencies (the extrasocial social). Philosophers represent such a group. They elaborate a particular code for reading texts and contexts. They situate themselves on a *cosmological* level that cannot be institutional. At least not in Greece. And not before Hegel.

Faced with the triple alliance of myth, ideology, and utopia, conflicts and contradictions are resolved by magic: they are consigned to the past or put off until the future.

They show up in works of art. How can we understand Greek tragedy? The political city, whether small town or organized urban core, seizes its conflictual relationship with the countryside, with its own countryside. It returns to the themes that have been lived and played out by the peasantry; it gives them another meaning. The city gives birth to the Apollonian spirit; the countryside gives birth to Dionysus. The scene of the massacred god who is devoured by his followers becomes a second-order event; it is reproduced or repeated at an assigned location for the re-presentation of malefic forces. On the stage of the theater, the City, home of the Logos and Apollonian force, exorcises chthonic violence by means of a controlled act of mimesis. The distance afforded by re-presentation and cathartic repetition serves as a buffer for those threatened by the danger of Dionysiac forces. It offers them a glimpse of the future of the City. The tragedians composed for the glory of Athena, in order to resolve the dilemma of law against custom, of justice against violence, of the individual against a brutal community. The succession of tragedians (Aeschylus, Sophocles, Euripides) can only be understood in this way, including the disappointment and bitterness that accompany them.[1] So many threats weigh upon the ancient city. Tragic themes are attributed to the urban, just as agricultural themes have been absorbed by the City. But these are not myths. Moreover, how could *urban myths* exist before the enormous shift that pushed society as a whole over to the side of urban reality, while diminishing the specific weight of agriculture, rural life, and the problems faced by the peasantry? From this moment on, the modern city began to take shape. It wrote itself into its blueprints and created a new identity for itself through its dreams, confessions, novels, and melodramas. Rural elements—myths, ideologies, utopias—are here taken up again as signifying units used with a different meaning. In Rousseau the City is a place of decay or corruption—in other words, civilization. It is contrasted with nature the way inequality is compared with equality and wealth with moderation. Jean-Jacques Rousseau thinks and works inside ideology, on the institutional level. Which is why he is important. Sometimes he makes use of myth, but rarely. This stripping of peasant themes from their context and initial meaning, this transformation of the ancient myths into an urban mythology, is more obvious in Restif de la Bretonne than it is in Rousseau. His unsettling work is entirely mythic and utopian (not ideological according to the definitions given previously, because it doesn't justify or refute any institutions but tends to ignore them), which is the source of its limitations and the reason for its greatness. Isn't it astonishing that at the very moment the physiocrats are beginning to theorize about the waning supremacy of nature and the countryside over the city, where this mixture of ideology and formal knowledge lags social practice, the mixture of myth and utopia goes deeper and farther, simultaneously announcing what is and what will be?

Around the middle of the eighteenth century, Nature, as image and concept, nostalgia and hope, came into view, in opposition to the City. At the same time, music, that is, harmony, dethroned architecture as the leading art of its time. Yet, a century later, the City dethroned Nature. The re-presentation of nature could no longer be elaborated except through, by, and for urban reality, which emerged as such. Nature was reduced to being a vehicle for regret, melancholy, and seasonal decoration. If we return to an analysis of dimensions, we could say that the symbolic dimension of the City was discovered by Victor Hugo, its paradigmatic dimension by Baudelaire, and its syntagmatic dimension by the many poets who inhabited the city and wrote about their travels: romantics and minor poets, from Gérard de Nerval to Lautréamont and Rimbaud. In this way, an image of the city tending toward a concept (that is toward an understanding) was discovered through myth, ideology, and utopia. And, remarkably, this took place, dimension by dimension, form after form. Hugo described and wrote of the symbols that could be read on buildings, in streets, even in sewers *(Notre-Dame de Paris, Les Misérables).* Baudelaire delivered and exposed a set of pertinent oppositions that characterized the urban (water and stone, immobile and mobile, the crowd and solitude). It is also worth noting that a large city, such as Paris, where the opposition to nature is so strong, has already entered the period of expansion. Baudelaire was present for the transformation of Paris through Haussmann's urbanism, the way Rimbaud was present for the Commune, an urban revolution. Ideology and utopia were already part of narrative, a form of description that was enriched by mythic themes. Paradise was no longer located in Nature, in the origin that preceded original sin. Through nostalgia, an artificial paradise (Baudelaire) supplanted a natural paradise, yet these artificial paradises are clearly urban. Although nature supplies certain elements of this paradise—wine and drugs, fabrics and metals, carnal desire and violence—reuse alters their meaning.

The urban looms on the horizon as form and light (an illuminating virtuality), as an ongoing practice, and as the source and foundation of another nature or a nature that is different from the initial nature. This takes places through mixed re-presentations that are too quickly dissociated here in this brief analysis: myth and utopia, ideology and science. The urban problematic announces its presence. What will come of this witches' cauldron, this dramatic intensification of creative powers and violence, this generalized exchange in which we no longer see what is being exchanged except when it is all around us: money, outsize and vulgar passions, desperate subtlety? The city affirms its presence and bursts apart. The urban asserts itself, not as some metaphysical entity, but as a unit based on practice. World and Cosmos, the old themes of philosophy, meet in action in the city, or rather, in the urban: the World, a path through shadows; the Cosmos, a harmonious scaffold with illuminated contours. Poetry no longer celebrates the beauty of the cosmos, its admirable "economy"—or the hieroglyph of the mind, the meaning of the path taken through shadows, through a tunnel or tortuous corridor. The poetic work becomes the "self-fulfillment of origin in beginning" (Maurice Blanchot). The scholar's path is the same as the poet's.

What is there to be said today about Haussmann's urbanism that hasn't already been said? He gutted Paris according to plan, deported the proletariat to the periphery of the city, simultaneously creating the suburb and the habitat, the gentrification, depopulation, and decay of the center. I would, however, like to emphasize certain aspects of this urbanist attitude. It harbors a logic that is inherent in class strategy and tends to maximize this type of rational coherence, which originated with Napoleon I and the absolute state. Haussmann cut through the urban fabric, was implacable in inscribing straight lines throughout the city. This isn't exactly the dictatorship of the right angle promulgated by the Bauhaus and Le Corbusier, but is already a regime governed by straight lines, alignment, and geometric perspective. This kind of rationality can only come from an institution. And in this case it was the highest, the supreme institution, the State, that intervened. It emphasized a tendency that originated in antiquity, in Rome, and through Rome, the Orient. Ever since its origins, the State expressed itself through the void: empty space, broad avenues, plazas of gigantic proportions open to spectacular processions. Bonapartism simply carried on the tradition by applying it to a historic city, to a highly complex urban space. And it altered the city immediately. It determined its logic, strategy, and rationality. To Napoleon's contemporaries, the ideology that underlay and supported that rationality and made it seem absolute looked very different. Most of them admired it. Those who were more reticent were aggrieved; they had lost the picturesque, they had lost hope. But they were old-fashioned. No doubt those who longed for the past were criticized because they also mourned the destruction of hovels in Paris. And their critics were not entirely wrong. However, the truth (the fragmentation of the city through gentrification) was hardly apparent to their contemporaries. What would it have taken for the truth to become apparent? The Commune, considered as a revolutionary urban practice, with its myth and ideology, its utopia (decentralization, Proudhonian federalism). The workers, chased from the center of the city to its outskirts, returned to the center occupied by the bourgeoisie. Through a combination of force, luck, and good timing, they took control of it.

Socialism, when it attempts to predict or imagine the future (which Marx refused to do, since he conceived of a *path*, not a *model*), provides us merely with an improved form of labor (salaries and material conditions on the job). But to offer nothing more would be shortsighted. For socialism soon finds itself confronted by the urban problematic, armed with nothing but childish concepts and ideologies. The labor and socialist movement has not yet been comparatively examined from this point of view. What effect, for example, did urban problems have on the various parties? Or on the Second and Third International? Municipal socialism, shortsighted, lacking a vision, failed miserably, even faster and more miserably than state socialism, which did not produce socialism (in Marx's sense) but large, powerful states. What did the "municipal socialists" accomplish, then? Their architects built subsidized housing projects. They "precipitated" (condensed) class relations within capitalism. Which proves that the reformists approached a problem that had not yet reached its current state of maturity and scope through the eyes of reform. How was this problem studied, resolved—or not resolved—in the Soviet Union after the October revolution? Or in the so-called socialist countries after the Second World War? Or in China during its ongoing revolution? Why is it that the Commune was not conceived as an *urban revolution* but as a revolution of an industrial proletariat moving toward industrialization, which does not correspond to historical truth?

I can only touch on such historical and political questions here. It appears that a nascent and uncertain socialism failed to avoid myth or ideology or utopia. Socialist thought, filled with self-confidence and never at a loss for dogmatic statements, claimed to transcend the town-country separation along with the division of labor into intellectual and manual labor, just as it believed it could transcend the market, money, the law of value, profitability, and so forth.

How can we overcome the town-country dichotomy? Through the disappearance of large cities, by scattering businesses throughout the countryside. The antiurban urbanist movement made its debut shortly after the October revolution, according to Anatole Kopp.[2] Although it resulted in projects remarkable for their architecture, it failed as an urban project. Soviet cities continue to grow in terms of size, productivity, and political importance to this day. In other words, in spite of the efforts of utopian thinkers at the exact moment when they thought they were being most realist and rational, the urban revolution in socialist countries proceeded without a conception of the urban that differed in any significant way from what was found in capitalist countries. Their political projects follow a distinctly anti-city line. And this is true even today, in Cuba and elsewhere.

Some have claimed that the cultural revolution in China will eliminate the difference between city and country, between the agricultural laborer and the industrial laborer, between manual and intellectual labor. Their approach resembles that of Marx and Soviet ideological claims. There is little novelty, however, in sending intellectuals to the country-side for a dose of manual labor, to work in fields or neigh-boring factories. Does this overcome the division of labor? Hardly. Can the revolutionary project be realized without advanced technology? Wouldn't the extension of the urban fabric, the disappearance of the countryside and agricultural labor as such, be accompanied by industrialization, mecha-nization, and overall automation? So that, at this level, over-coming the earlier situation would assume a new meaning? In the meantime, Marxist-Leninist thought in China has denounced the city as a center of despotic power (which is not without an element of truth). The cities harbor bastions and fortresses directed against the peasantry. The large cit-ies, the headquarters of companies and banks, trading posts, human trading posts that attract millions of the hungry, would be destroyed. The global city, surrounded by a global countryside and peasantry, would serve as a background for revolutionary activity. As for the commune (in the Chinese sense), it would serve as a means, a step along the road to the urbanization of the countryside and the ruralization of the cities. The commune supposedly has hospitals and schools, centers of culture, commerce, and leisure. There are no shan-ties, there is no overpopulation. The commune alone can assimilate the groups that compose it and the individuals who compose those groups into a collective "we." It avoids sedentarism as well as nomadism. Technology is no longer destructive but collectively controlled. Power has limits. The Chinese commune would be capable of replacing the old feminine city, protective and passive, as well as the old mas-culine city, active and oppressive. At least that's what certain defenders of the "anti-city" project claim.

Their argument can be contested on several grounds, for it is not only ideological and political (in the short term used to promote a given policy or short-term policies), but utopian in a conventional sense. In China today, as in the

Soviet Union yesterday, cities continue to grow along with the economy and, possibly, the increase in speed. As they do elsewhere. The demographic, ideological, and sociological reasons, the economic and political advantages of the city, are the same in China as elsewhere. Long-term global urbanization is under way. The urban space is no differently defined in a socialist country than it is anywhere else. The urban problematic, urbanism as ideology and institution, urbanization as a worldwide trend, are global facts. The urban revolution is a planetary phenomenon.

Moreover, if the "global city" is of interest to the theoreticians of the "Chinese way," the eventual "suburbanization" of a large part of the world is of no less interest to urban strategy. Can such a strategy assume, however, that the countryside will encircle the city, that peasant guerrillas will lead the assault on urban centers? Today, such a vision or conception of the class struggle on a global scale appears old-fashioned. The revolutionary capacity of the peasantry is not on the rise; it is being readsorbed, although not consistently. On the contrary, a kind of overall colonization of space by "decision-making centers" seems to be taking shape. Centers of wealth and information, of knowledge and power, are beginning to create feudal dependencies. In this case, the boundary line does not divide city and country but cuts across the urban phenomenon, between a dominated periphery and a dominating center.

Globalization and the planetary nature of the urban phenomenon—specifically, the urban problematic and critical phase—appeared in science fiction novels before they were revealed to our understanding (or through that ambiguous blend of ideology and knowledge that we analyze under the name of urbanism). In science fiction, optimistic predictions of the urban phenomenon are rare; pessimism is much more common. The ideology inherent in these mythic stories often extends the imperatives of industrial planning, without clarifying all the implications of the urban phenomenon. Nonetheless, this general pessimism is part of the problematic. In science fiction, the city of the future is broken; it proliferates as a disease afflicting humanity and space, a medium for vice, deformation, and violence.

For the moment, we can only acknowledge the multiplicity of lexical items (readings) associated with the urban phenomenon. The myth has filled a void: knowledge that is oriented toward and by practice. It continues to occupy that place, mixed with utopia and ideology. There are various ways of reading this highly complex phenomenon. There is a *morphological* reading (practiced by the geographer and possibly the urbanist). There is a *technological* reading, practiced by the administrator, the politician looking for a means of intervention. There is a reading of the *possible* (and the *impossible*) that provides us with an image of the variations of finite existence—that of the human being—supplied by urban life in place of the traditional unity that encloses "drives" and values within its narrow boundaries. Perhaps the mythic tale, formerly the medium of the philosopher and poet, and now of the science-fiction novelist, combines the various "lexical items" associated with the urban phenomenon, without worrying too much about classifying them according to their provenance or signification. Perhaps this narrative is less reductive than the fragmentary readings and understandings it makes use of by detaching them from their context and their isolation. Perhaps it projects an image of the urban problematic only by dissimulating its contradictions. The scenario of the future has yet to be determined.

6 || Urban Form

What exactly is the essence, or substance, of the urban phenomenon? Until now, I have not provided a definition based on substance or content. The associated functions, structures, and forms (in the usual sense of the word), although necessary, have not appeared sufficient to define the term. We have cataloged, located, and observed the growth over time of the political and administrative function, the commercial function, the productive function (artisanal, manufacturing, industrial) within the classical city. These functions have a twofold character: with respect to the territory that urban centers administer, dominate, and cover with networks, and with respect to the city itself, which is administered, dominated (to the extent that it is and because it is dominating), and integrated with networks of production and distribution. The characteristic of the urban phenomenon is obviously located at the juncture of these twofold functions, their point of articulation. Therefore, simply listing those functions serves little purpose. Their description, their detailed analysis breaks apart, depending on the discipline (economy, politics, sociology), without ever achieving that

115

articulation. Analysis only makes sense if it is able to distinguish organizations and institutions, to the extent that they control the exterior and interior functions of the city and can therefore combine them. Structures are also twofold: they are *morphological* (sites and situations, buildings, streets and squares, monuments, neighborhoods) and *sociological* (distribution of the population, ages and sexes, households, active or passive population, socioprofessional categories, managers and the managed). As for its form in the conventional sense of the word, that is to say geometric or plastic, there is a spatial element that must be accounted for—grid or radial-concentric. However, such an arrangement does not become obvious unless we turn our attention to circulation, unless we restrict the urban problematic to the problems of circulation. The invention of new forms (X-shaped, spiral, helical, concave, etc.) is merely a simplistic solution to the urban problematic.

As we have seen, the essential aspect of the urban phenomenon is its centrality, but a *centrality* that is understood in conjunction with the dialectical movement that creates or destroys it. The fact that any point can become central is the meaning of urban space-time. However, centrality is not indifferent to what it brings together, for it requires a content. And yet, the exact nature of that content is unimportant. Piles of objects and products in warehouses, mounds of fruit in the marketplace, crowds, pedestrians, goods of various kinds, juxtaposed, superimposed, accumulated—this is what makes the urban urban. If the city is always a spectacle for itself, viewed from high on a terrace, a tower, a hilltop, a vantage point (a high point that is the *elsewhere* where the urban reveals itself), it is not because the spectator perceives a picture that is outside reality, but because her glance is consolidating. It is the very form of the urban, revealed. Everything that occurs within the urban reality does so as if everything that constituted that reality could be compared, and always increasingly so. In this way—in confusion—the urban is conceived, perceived, and revealed. Agriculture settles into nature. It produces according to the laws of physis, guiding nature along rather than forcing it into shape. If physis moves from the seed to the flower and the fruit, beginning the cycle again, peasant space and time do not break the cycle; they are integral to it, they depend closely on its particularities: the composition of the soil, spontaneous flora and fauna, biological equilibriums, microclimates. Industry captures nature but doesn't respect it. It exhausts its energies, rips it apart to grab hold of its resources and raw materials, ravages it to "produce" things (exchangeable, salable) that are not in or of nature. Industry is not subjected to any given place but still depends on place. Although it tends to occupy the entirety of a territory, it does so only by combining a number of dispersed fragments, companies, through the market.

The city is vastly different. Indeed, it is not only a devouring activity, consumption; it becomes productive (means of production) but initially does so by bringing together the elements of production. It combines markets (the inventory includes the market for agricultural and industrial products—local, regional, national, global: capital markets, labor markets, markets for the land itself, for signs and symbols). The city brings together whatever is engendered somewhere else, by nature or labor: fruits and objects, products and producers, works and creations, activities and situations. What does the city create? Nothing. It centralizes creation. And yet it creates everything. Nothing exists without exchange, without union, without proximity, that is, without relationships. The city creates a situation, the urban situation, where *different* things occur one after another and do not exist separately but according to their differences. The urban, which is indifferent to each difference it contains, often seems to be as indifferent as nature, but with a cruelty all its own. However, the urban is not indifferent to all differences, precisely because it unites them. In this sense, the city constructs, identifies, and delivers the essence of social relationships: the reciprocal existence and manifestation of differences arising from or resulting in conflicts. Isn't this the justification and meaning of this rational delirium known as the city, the urban? (Social) relationships continue to deteriorate based on the distance, time, and space that separate institutions and groups. They are revealed in the (virtual) negation of that distance. This is the source of the latent violence inherent in the urban, as well as the equally disturbing character of celebrations and holidays. Immense crowds gather along the unstable border between joyous frenzy and cruel frenzy, trancelike in the grip of ludic enjoyment. Rarely does a celebration occur without some kind of "happening," some unforeseen movement of the crowd, people fainting, trampled underfoot, dying. Centrality, an aspect of mathematics, is also an aspect of drama. It unites them the way it unites *everything*, including symbols and signs (including those of union). The signs of the urban are the signs of assembly: the things that promote assembly (the street and its surface, stone, asphalt, sidewalks) and the requirements for assembly (seats, lights). The urban is most forcefully evoked by the constellation of lights at night, especially when flying over a city—the dazzling impression of brilliance, neon, street signs, streetlights, incitements of various kinds, the simultaneous accumulation of wealth and signs. But during its realization, this concentration flexes and cracks. It requires another center, a periphery, an elsewhere. An other and different place. This movement, produced by the urban, in turn produces the urban. Creation comes to a halt to create again.

The urban is, therefore, pure form: a place of encounter, assembly, simultaneity. This form has no specific content, but is a center of attraction and life. It is an abstraction, but unlike a metaphysical entity, the urban is a concrete abstraction, associated with practice. Living creatures, the products of industry, technology and wealth, works of culture, ways of living, situations, the modulations and ruptures of the everyday—the urban *accumulates* all content. But it is more than and different from accumulation. Its contents (things, objects, people, situations) are mutually exclusive because they are diverse, but inclusive because they are brought together and imply their mutual presence. The urban is both form and receptacle, void and plenitude, superobject and nonobject, supraconsciousness and the totality of consciousnesses. It is associated with the *logic of form* and with the *dialectic of content* (with the differences and contradictions of content). It is associated with mathematical form (in the urban, everything is calculable, quantifiable, programmable; everything, that is, except the drama that results from the co-presence and re-presentation of the elements calculated, quantified, and programmed), with geometrical form (gridded, circular), and therefore with symmetry and recurrence (paths are reversible, in spite of the irreversibility of time, and, consequently, *legible,* urban simultaneity being analogous with literature, with the rational order of coexisting elements). And yet, in spite of its socio-logic, the urban does not constitute a system. There is neither an urban system nor an incursion of the urban into a unitary system of forms, because of the (relative) independence between form and content. This precludes a definition of the urban phenomenon (the urban) in terms of a system or as a system. It also precludes defining it as an object (substance) or subject (consciousness). It is a *form.* Because of this, it tends toward

1. *centrality,* through distinct modes of production, different productive relations—a trend that has already affected the "decision-making centers," the embodiment of the state, along with all the attendant dangers associated with such a movement—and
2. *polycentrality,* omnicentrality, the rupture of the center,

dispersion—a trend that can be oriented either toward the
constitution of different centers (analogous and possibly
complementary) or toward dispersion and segregation.

Few would argue with the difficulty in understanding, much
less mastering, such a contradictory movement. But this
is hardly sufficient grounds for denying its existence and
substituting either a simplified socio-logic (a "pure" logic
of form) or the emphasis on a given content (the industrial
production of exchangeable objects such as merchandise, the
circulation of information, authoritarian decisions, automobile circulation, and so on).

Dialectical reason, both mental and social, inherent in
urban form and its relationship to its content, can explain
certain aspects of the urban. There are no urban "forms" in
the plastic (rather than logical) sense, silhouettes against a
dark background, like those that stand out against a natural
backdrop and make manifest the obscurity of that background. Abundance, proliferation—everything is distin-
guishable. Elements that are called or summoned blend into
one another. Everything is legible. Urban space is transparent. Everything signifies, even if signifiers float freely, since
everything is related to "pure" form, is contained in that
form. Order and form tend to blur together, even though
form is simultaneously perceived, conceived, and made
manifest (dreamed). But *we* (subjects, individuals or groups,
who are also in and of the urban reality and collected there
the way things are) realize that this transparency is deceptive.
The city, the urban, is also mysterious, occult. Alongside the
strident signs of visible power such as wealth and the police,
plots are engineered and hidden powers conspire, behind appearances and beneath the transparency. Until the arrival of
a new order, the urban will never lack an element of repression, which arises from what is hidden within it and the will
to keep hidden the dramas, the latent violence, death, and the

quotidian. This repressive side of the urban is incorporated in the conception of space; it supports transgression. Here, the relation between transparency and opacity differs from what it was either in nature or in industry. Couldn't it be said that there exists a dialectical relationship, a difference in contradiction? Social opacity tends to manifest itself, to appear as mental clarity. If truth is hidden and loses its meaning, the meaning of truth can fracture at any moment. Or explode. Yet urban life hovers, ambiguous and uncertain, between the interpretation of messages based on a (recognized) code and the metalanguage that is content to paraphrase messages that are known, repeated, redundant. The city writes itself on its walls and in its streets. But that writing is never completed. The book never ends and contains many blank or torn pages. It is nothing but a draft, more a collection of scratches than writing. Course and discourse accompany one another but never meet. Can the urban paradigm, namely the set of pertinent oppositions that give meaning to things (center and noncenter, information and redundancy, open and closed, public and nonpublic) ever find closure? Apparently not. Certain oppositions, like particularity and difference, which resolutely reflect lived experience, prevent that set from ever terminating. The city and the urban, super-objects and super-signs, are not exactly based on the same concepts as objects and signs. And yet they imply and contain them, both objects and signs and the concepts that refer to those objects and signs. To understand the laws governing objects and signs in urban reality, we need to add to those concepts (system, set, division and arrangement, the sociology of groups and groupings) specific concepts such as "network" (of exchange, communication). For the urban is *also* defined as the juxtaposition and superimposition of networks, the assembly and union of those networks, some of which are constituted on the basis of the territory, some on industry, and others on the basis of other centers within the urban fabric.

In this way the notion of a "rupture" (a relative discontinuity) between the urban and its precedents, the industrial and agricultural spheres, is made concrete. Upon closer examination, this rupture turns out to be not epistemological or philosophical, not even and not solely political or historical. It goes much deeper than that. It simultaneously introduces and grounds a form of knowledge, a field. Space and time change, of course, but what distinguishes them is the introduction of a form (within a form) similar to logical form and *almost as abstract and active* as that logical form (which is associated with language, discourse, reasoning, analysis, effective action), as abstract and active as the form of exchange (of value and commodities) but different. This form relegates certain outmoded contents to the past; it acts *selectively* through knowledge and the results (or residues) of history. It absorbs other contents as well, combines them *actively* in a totality or virtual synthesis, which does not need philosophy for its fulfillment but can simply be recognized as a channel (strategy) for action. If we want to understand this form and the modalities of its intervention, there is no point in starting with space as such (since it is reconsidered, reworked) or time as such (since it is transformed). It is *form* itself, as generator of a virtual object, the urban, the encounter and assembly of all objects and subjects, existing or possible, that must be explored. As with conquered space and accumulated time, we must also abandon as a starting point philosophy, ideological and institutional discourse, the customary scientificity that limits thought to an existing framework and prevents it from exploring possibilities through form. And, most important, we must exclude conventional models, which have generally been adopted, from industrialization, productionism, and economism. Where then do we begin? We begin with a formal conception of logic and a dialectic of content (including that fundamental content, the base, the foundation that is everywhere the same and never the same, always other and never other: *desire,* which, with an overwhelming degree of competence and cunning, is able to make use of form to recognize itself and be recognized, to confront itself and struggle in the urban).

In this way the space-time axis, extending from the zero point of urban reality to the completion of the process (industrialization, urbanization), assumes meaning and scope. Initially, when near the zero point, the urban was merely a work in progress, a seed—somewhat like a tool, a stone or wooden club, or language and concepts the first time they were used to identify a place. With the first gathering and collection of objects existing separately in nature, from the first cairn or pile of fruit, *centrality* came into being, and with it its virtual realization. From the very first, combining, assembling, and gathering were essential elements of social practice; it was a rational aspect of production that did not coincide with productive activity but was not dissociated from it, either. This conception of a center differs from the reality that is manifest in nature, but also from the social aspects of agricultural and industrial activity. These are not based on the virtual cancellation (negation) of distance in time and space, on action and effort in this sense. Yet the concept retains certain physical notions because it is associated with logico-mathematical concepts, although it cannot be equated with them.

Physicists also conceive of a concentration of matter scattered throughout the cosmos at a single point, the density of this matter becoming infinite and the distances (voids and spaces) between molecules and particles canceling one another out. This impossibility clarifies the real. The urban assumes cosmic significance; it is globalized (combining the *world* as obscure path and *cosmos* as luminous unity). Science fiction often describes this cosmic aspect of the City, a rediscovered physical space, modeled as an artifact of the urban. Through the succession of cities and their types, the urban, already present as virtuality in the germinal stage, becomes concrete—but has no need of metaphysical support or transcendent unity. The political city, the mercantile city, the industrial city have this twofold quality: a process that engenders the urban (and is shaped by the urban) coupled with provisional limits inflicted on this process by the conditions of agricultural and industrial production. Through this dialectical movement, the urban reacts to what has preceded it, grows out of it, and serves as its terminus, without this implying any sense of metaphysical finality. Here, too, the formless, the dispersed, the scattered assume form. That form affirms itself as an end; we must rely on knowledge to control the process. The unifying power of urban form is not infinite. In fact it re-presents the summum of the finite: finitude. This form, which is itself empty (similar to "pure" logical form, or tautology), does not participate in the infinite power attributed to divinity, the transcendent Idea, absolute Reason. The urban, because it combines finite elements in finite places and in the finitude of place (point, center), is itself finite. It can perish. It is threatened by insignificance and, especially, the power of political society. Urban form does tend to break the limits that try to circumscribe it. Its movement seeks a path. But it is not immediately obvious that any obstacles will be sidestepped or overcome. The dialectic (contradictory) character of this movement means that it can be thwarted, means that certain elements can be used against the movement of the whole. The urban, a place of drama, can be transformed into the drama of the urban. Can segregation, the enemy of assemblies and encounters, arrest this movement? Can uniform space, without "topoi," without places, without contrast, pure indifference, a caricature of the relation between the urban and its components, stifle urban reality? It can. It can even assume a mantle of democracy. Urban democracy would imply an equality of places, equal participation in global exchanges. Centrality would produce hierarchy and therefore inequality. And yet, wouldn't dispersion result in segregation? Can revolutionary upheaval break the boundaries of urban reality? Sometimes it can. Which is a measure of the importance of a radical critique of separation, segregation, the politics of space, and, more generally, urbanism.

The above helps give meaning and scope to the theory of *differential space*. The differences that are established in space do not come from space as such but from that which settles there, that which is assembled and confronted by and in the urban reality. Contrasts, oppositions, superpositions, and juxtapositions replace separation, spatio-temporal distances. The theory goes something like this: Space (and space-time) changes with the period, sphere, field, and dominant activity. There are, therefore, three layers in space: rural space, industrial space, and urban space, superposed, telescoped, sometimes absorbed into one another. At the start of the agrarian period, a given space (thoughts of and in urban space can think this "given" as such, as pure nature, as geography, but they can no longer achieve it without reconstructing it) was marked out, oriented, hierarchized. The initial topoi, or place-names, once given a name, entered a binary grid that was mental and social, practical and verbal. These places (topoi) were an immediate product of nature: the particularities of the soil (material nature, flora and fauna, the appearance of paths and byways) served as names. In place of the heterogeneity of the natural environment, industrial space substituted homogeneity, or rather, its will to homogeneity, consistent with its quantitative rationality. In a planned space these topoi were mere accidents, vague commodities of a folkloric language; all places were homologous, distinct only in their distance from one another. Objective and measurable, space was represented only with reference to productivist criteria. While there is an advantage in con-solidating all the social functions of production, it is not al-ways possible to do so. In the first place, when it is possible, we end up with the urban phenomenon. In the second, there are additional costs: the cost of space, the displacement of objects and information. Methods of optimization can, in principle, modify the use of space. They add a scientific ve-neer to the project of industrial rationality: the extension on a global scale of the internal organization of the enterprise, of the "industrial division of labor." These methods are in-different to the urban phenomenon but are incorporated in it every time we succeed in bringing together production and markets (labor, capital, products).

This urban space differs radically from industrial space, precisely because it is differential (and not homogeneous). Even if the initial property boundaries and rural names re-main, urban space radically reshapes them. Oppositions and contrasts replace solitary particularities (relative to the soil). Consider the map of Paris. Many of the names have rural origins (Butte-aux-Cailles, Grange-Batelière, Moulin-Vert). We know that the streets in the Latin Quarter follow the trace of rural footpaths and roads, which the people of Paris took to go to their prairies, vineyards, and fields on the Left Bank. Over the centuries, however, this network turned into a labyrinth, the center of the intelligentsia and its ferment, which contrasted with the commercial roadways and grid-like projections of state order. Haussmann succeeded in cut-ting up the Latin Quarter but failed to exterminate this op-position. The retail space around Les Halles was established along a north-south axis and was filled with artisanal and manufacturing products. This social group led the assault in extending itself toward the east of Paris, until then inhabited by the aristocracy (the Marais) and royalty (near the Bastille, the Arsenal, etc.). The east-west axis along the Seine was never fully established, even after massive industrialization. The site, the situation explain why. Even though the river, a neutral urban space, served as a means of transport for centuries, the north-south axis had a preponderant importance economically, militarily, and politically. The contrast was remarkable. The east-west axis, between Vincennes and Place de la Concorde, was marked by esplanades that were built away from local circulation, except for the most recent (Concorde, Place de l'Étoile). They served as meeting places and were the setting for festivals, games, and promenades: Place Royale (Place des Vosges), Place des Victoires, Palais-Royal, Place Vendôme. In contrast, the Louvre is the starting point for the triumphal way that leads westward. Although originally a noncommercial route, it became a site for the deployment of royal and imperial splendor (Tuileries, Place Louis XV, Cours-la-Reine, Champs-Élysées, and later l'Étoile). In this way, the thrust and pressure of the major social groups model space differentially, even when we would expect homogeneity (in the case of a large capital city such as Paris). Quite remarkably, there are no esplanades or squares along the north-south axis (Rue Saint-Denis, Rue Saint-Martin, Boulevard Saint-Michel, and Rue Saint-Jacques) other than intersections.

It's not the "élan vital" of the urban community that explains the structures of space, as Marcel Poëte expressed in the language of Bergson. It is the result of a history that must be conceived as the work of social "agents" or "actors," of collective "subjects" acting in successive thrusts, discontinuously (relatively) releasing and fashioning layers of space. These major social groups, comprising classes and fractions of classes, as well as institutions that cannot be adequately defined in terms of class character (royalty or municipality, for example), act with and/or against one another. From their interactions, their strategies, successes, and failures arise the qualities and "properties" of urban space. The general form of the urban encompasses these various differences by bringing them together. If Paris is any example, the proletariat has not yet created a space. The merchant bourgeoisie, the intellectuals, and politicians modeled the city. The industrialists demolished it. The working class never had any space other than that of its expropriation, its deportation: segregation.

I referred to those parts of space that were comparable, that could be discussed and read (on maps, along trajectories, in images that had been more or less elaborated by "subjects") in a way that afforded direct comparison, as isotopies. For example, there is a remarkable isotopy in the spaces created by state rationalism: long straight lines, broad avenues, voids, empty perspectives, an occupation of the soil that makes a clean break with its antecedents, without regard for either the rights and interests of the lower classes or cost. These traits are distinct: from the Parisian spaces ordered by the kings to those commanded by the empire to those of the republics. They continue to expand, except in one respect: their mediocrity, their conscious and increasingly visible subordination to the needs of monopoly industry, as we follow the recent axis that has commercialized and industrialized the ancient royal and imperial way. No longer do units of production inhabit urban space, modeling it in a way that, although it can be contested, is at least straightforward. There is nothing but offices, one after the other.

Isotopies: places of identity, identical places. Neighboring order. Heterotopy: the other place, the place of the other, simultaneously excluded and interwoven. Distant order. Between them there are neutral spaces: crossroads, thoroughfares, places that are not so much nothing as indifferent (neutral). Often these are cuts/sutures (like the broad street or avenue that simultaneously separates and joins two neighborhoods, two contrasting heterotopies). Spaces marked by different functions are superimposed on one another. Isotopy is associated with multifunctionality (formerly embodied in plazas). Animated environments, especially streets, are multifunctional (passage, commerce, entertainment). In the case of small streets, the suture is more important than the cut, and the reverse is true for large thoroughfares and highways, which crisscross and slice through urban space. The isotopy-heterotopy difference can only be understood dynamically. In urban space, something is always happening. Relations change. Differences and contrasts can result in conflict, or are attenuated, erode, or corrode.

Urban space as a whole was heterotopic compared with rural space until the reversal that began in the sixteenth century in Europe, which resulted in the invasion of the countryside by the urban fabric. During this same period, the outlying areas remained strongly heterotopic. Crisscrossed by long, poorly equipped thoroughfares, ambiguous spaces, they harbored populations from different origins: cart drivers and mercenaries, traders, seminomads forced to settle outside the city limits, often suspect and sacrificed in time of war. After a time, the city began to merge with these outlying areas, to assimilate them by annexing them to its more active neighborhoods, inhabited by merchants and artisans. This led to urban agglomeration and the ensuing strong sense of popular unity that is solidified by struggles with a monarchical state. It wasn't until the rise of the bourgeoisie that this trend reversed. Popular elements were expelled from the center to still rural peripheral heterotopies, which have since been changed into "suburbs," habitat receptacles, typified by a highly visible form of isotopy. In this sense, heterotopy corresponds—but to a limited extent—to the anomie discussed by sociologists. Anomic groups construct heterotopic spaces, which are eventually reclaimed by the dominant praxis.

What about u-topia, the non-place, the place for that which doesn't occur, for that which has no place of its own, that is always elsewhere? On a map of Paris (the so-called Turgot map of approximately 1735), u-topia can be neither read nor seen, and yet it is there in all its glory. It is where the gaze that overlooks the large city is situated, a vaguely determined place, but one that is carefully conceived and imagined (imaged), a place of consciousness; that is, a consciousness of totality. In general, this place, imagined and real, is found near the borders of verticality, the dimension of desire, power, and thought. Sometimes it is found deep within the subterranean city imagined by the novelist or poet, the underside of the city given over to conspiracy and crime. U-topia combines near and distant orders.

In terms of its relationship to content, urban form creates the contradiction (dialectic) previously mentioned, which I would now like to discuss in greater detail. Earlier, I noted that something is always happening in urban space. The void, the nothingness of action, can only be apparent; neutrality is a limiting case. The void (a place) attracts; it has this sense and this end. Virtually, anything can happen anywhere. A crowd can gather, objects can pile up, a festival unfold, an event—terrifying or pleasant—can occur. This is why urban space is so fascinating: centrality is always possible. At the same time, this space can empty itself, expel its content, become a place of pure scarcity or power. It is grasped in terms of its fixed structures, staged, hierarchized, from the apartment building to the urban in its entirety, defined by visible limits or the invisible limits of administrative decrees and orders. It can easily be divided into parties and partitions, into basic objects and units. While it may be fascinating because of its availability, it is equally fascinating because of the arbitrariness of its predefined units (along with office blocks and residential neighborhoods, there are arrondissements, the bureaucratic limits of electoral districts, etc.).

To resolve this contradiction, we can imagine the complete mobilization, not of the population, but of space. A space taken over by the ephemeral. So that every place becomes multifunctional, polyvalent, transfunctional, with an incessant turnover of functions; where groups take control of spaces for expressive actions and constructions, which are soon destroyed. (An admirable example of such a conjuncturally modeled space, modified by group action, is the large exhibition space, especially the one in Montreal. An ephemeral city rose up from a transformed site, a magnificent city, where everydayness was absorbed in festival, where the urban was transparent in its splendor.)

In this way, u-topia, an illuminating virtuality already present, will absorb and metamorphose the various topoi.

U-topia is as necessary as isotopy and heterotopy. It is everywhere and nowhere. The transcendence of desire and power, the immanence of the people, the omnipresence of symbolism and the imaginary, the rational and dreamlike vision of centrality accumulating wealth and human gestures, the presence of the other, presence-absence, the need for a presence that is never achieved—these are also the characteristics of differential space. Urban form unites these differences, whether minimal or maximal. This form is defined only in and through this consolidating unity of difference (all differences, that is to say, differences forming a whole). This consolidation implies three terms, three topoi: isotopy, heterotopy, and u-topia. However, the transcendence of utopia and the overwhelming nature of monumentality and the void (enormous plazas, nocturnal squares), which embody the u-topic, require closer scrutiny. This does not imply unexamined praise for this element, half-fictional, half-real, which would result in a form of urban idealism. This last point has already been touched upon: the u-topic appears as if it were incorporated in certain necessary spaces such as gardens and parks. It is impossible to consider these spaces as neutral (neutral elements of the urban spatial ensemble). Parks and gardens make the "elsewhere" sensible, visible, and legible, intercalated in urban time and place. They refer to a twofold utopia: absolute nature and pure facticity. When the (public) park and garden are no longer subject to a form of rationality whose origin is productivist and industrial, when they are no longer neutralized, no longer reduced to being "greenery," an avaricious and parodic geometry, they suggest an absolute and inaccessible nature—grottos, wind, altitude, the sea, islands—as well as facticity—the trimmed and tortured tree that serves as pure ornament. The garden, the park, are both, absolute contrasts that have been forced together, but in such a way that they evoke liberty, u-topian separation. Japan has many examples of the art of the garden. Paris does as well, but there they have very different qualities. Again, there is no urban space without utopian symbols, without a use of height and depth that is based on laws that are not those of utilitarian empiricism or a mediocre aesthetic borrowed from painting, sculpture, or any specific art, for that matter: these are the laws of urban form.

I have already said most of what I wanted to say about the relations between difference and particularity. Differential space retains particularities, which are experienced through the filter of homogeneous space. A selection is made. The particularities that are incompletely homogenized survive, are reestablished with a different meaning. This is the source of a major theoretical problem: the reuse of signifying units detached from their initial context. The problem has cropped up before in philosophy, ideology, and mythology. We come across it again in the discussion of space. Once again, the role of practice is critical. Only urban practice can resolve the problem, since it was urban practice that presented us with the problem in the first place.

In urban practice, discourse on or about the city is circumscribed, inscribed; it prescribes acts, directions. Can we claim that this practice is defined by a discourse? By speech or writing? The urban reality is the site of limitless speech only to the extent that it offers a finite, but large, number of pathways for its expression. This discourse incorporates earlier, natural, historic units. And although it is written and read, it is not exhausted by the writing and reading of urban texts.

It is worthwhile to discuss the confusion between *difference, distinction, separation,* and *segregation.* Difference is incompatible with segregation, which caricatures it. When we speak of difference, we speak of relationships, and therefore proximity relations that are conceived and perceived, and inserted in a twofold space-time order: near and distant. Separation and segregation break this relationship. They constitute a totalitarian order, whose strategic goal is to break down concrete totality, to break the urban. Segregation complicates and destroys complexity.

A result of the complexification of the social, the urban promotes practical rationality, the link between *form* and *information.* And what about synthesis? It is given in practice, to the extent that practice demands freedom of information, namely the possibility that every place, every event can inform the others and receive information from them in turn.

Difference is informing and informed. It produces form, the best form resulting from optimal information. Separation and segregation isolate information. They produce formlessness. The order they provide is merely apparent. Only an ideology can use it to counter the disorder of information, encounters, or centrality. Only a limited industrial or state rationalism can mutilate the urban by dissociating it, by projecting onto the terrain its "spectral analysis," composed of disjunct elements, where the exchange of information can no longer take place.

Now that we have a better understanding of urban form (including its practical aspect), I would like to turn to its concrete manifestation in the form of an urban strategy.[1]

7 || Toward an Urban Strategy

Contemporary theory would, to some extent, have been familiar to Marx. Radical criticism was already clearing a path to thought and action. Marx, as we know, used as his starting point German philosophy, English political economy, and contemporary French ideas about revolutionary action and its objectives (socialism). His critique of Hegelianism, economic science, and history and its meaning enabled Marx to conceive of capitalist society both as a totality and as a moment of total transformation. Negativity would give rise to a new form of optimism. For Marx the negativity of radical critique coincided, theoretically and practically, with that of the revolutionary proletariat. The similarities and differences between this situation and the second half of the twentieth century would soon become apparent. To the Marxist critique of philosophy and political ideology, we can now add the radical critique of the reductive disciplines, the fragmentary sciences, which have become specialized and institutionalized. Only through such critique can we distinguish the contribution of each of those sciences to the emerging totality. We now know that this is the only way to gain access to totality, rather than through a summation or juxtaposition of the "positive" results of those sciences. Taken alone, each of these sciences dissolves in fragments or confusion, dogmatism or nihilism.

The dialectic between urban form and content is such that (1) the existence of this form ensures a rationality of the "real," which can then be analyzed conceptually; (2) form, as such, becomes the basis for study at the highest level; (3) content is based on analyses that will further fragment this already diverse content: the fragmentary sciences. Consequently, what is needed is perpetual criticism (and self-criticism) of those sciences on behalf of rational (global) form.

A critique of the specialized sciences implies a critique of specialized politics, structures, and their ideologies. Every political group, and especially every structure, justifies itself through an ideology that it develops and nurtures: nationalism or patriotism, economism or state rationalism, philosophism, (conventional) liberal humanism. This tends to mask essential problems, primarily those associated with urban society and its mutation (transformation or revolution). These ideologies, which are ill-suited to the use to which they are put, were developed during an earlier period, a period characterized by industrial rationalism and the division of intellectual labor. Here I would again like to make use of the methodology of levels to distinguish tactics and strategies. We can state the following:

1. On the level of projects and plans, there is always some distance between elaboration and execution. In this context, we should make a distinction between demands and disputes, which are frequently confused. Disputes reveal the ideologies characteristic of the groups or classes involved, including the ideology (or ideologies) of those who contribute to the development of projects, *ideological urbanism*. The intervention of "disputants" introduces conflict into social logics (socio-logic as ideo-logic). The possibility of

dispues = urban democracy

dispute causes these logics to manifest themselves as ideologies and promotes confrontation, which is a measure of the degree of urban democracy. The passivity of those involved, their silence, their reticent prudence are an indication of the absence of urban democracy; that is, concrete democracy. Urban revolution and concrete (developed) democracy coincide. The urban practice of groups and classes—that is, their way of life, their morphology—can only confront urban ideology in this way. And, in this way, disputes evolve into demands.

2. On what we might call the epistemological level, we can raise the question of knowledge, formal or otherwise. In terms of the way the problematic has been defined, it seems unlikely that a "body" of acquired knowledge can be formed. The problematic will dominate scientificity until a new order arises. In other words, ideology and knowledge blend together, and we must continuously strive to distinguish them. Yet every science can consider itself a party to the understanding of the urban phenomenon, providing the following two conditions are met: that it provide specific concepts and a method, and that it abandon imperialism, a requirement that implies a continuous process of criticism and self-criticism.

There is no question that sociology brings with it a large number of specific concepts, such as "ideology" (together with its critical implications), "institution," and "anomie" and all that they imply. Obviously, this is not an exhaustive list, and I mention these concepts specifically only because they are exemplary subjects for criticism. Further discussion is needed to determine if some of the concepts developed by Georges Gurvitch—for example, "effervescent behavior" or the "plurality of time"—would be useful for the analysis of the urban phenomenon.[1] However, concepts and representations of centrality, the urban fabric, and urban space are not restricted to the field of sociology (although my comments should not be interpreted as a criticism of the concepts themselves).

On the highest theoretical level, we need to envisage the mutation (or transformation or revolution) through which so-called industrial society becomes urban society. Such mutations determine the problematic—that is, the problematic character of the real. Can we claim that the phenomena associated with industrialization within a given global framework (institutional, ideological) have been completely supplanted by urban phenomena? That the former are now subordinated to the latter? Not in my opinion. We shouldn't confuse trends with realization. Today's society is undergoing a transition and can best be understood in this sense. The phenomena and implications of industry are only now beginning to wane. On this level, we find that the so-called socialist countries were the first to transform their institutions to meet the needs of industrial production: modified rationality, planning, programming. In this, the capitalist countries have caught up to them—up to a certain point. The urban problematic is global, but the way we approach it depends on the economic, social, and political structure of the country, as well as its ideological superstructures. It is not obvious that these so-called socialist countries have shown as much initiative (more or less successful) in urbanization as they have in industrialization.

Knowledge of the urban phenomenon can only become a science in and through the conscious formation of an urban praxis, along with its own rationality, to supplant the now fully realized industrial praxis. Through this complex process, analysis can delineate "objects" or construct "models," all of which are provisional, all of which can be revised or criticized. This assumes the confrontation mentioned earlier between urban ideology and the urban practice of social groups and classes. It also assumes the intervention of social and political forces and the liberation of capacities for invention, without excluding the closest thing we have to utopianism, namely "pure" imagination.

I would again like to emphasize the need for a reversal of the conventional way of looking at things. The possibility of a strategy is in fact linked to this reversal, but the phase in which it is produced makes forecasts and projects difficult. In general, urbanization is represented as a consequence of industrialization, the dominant phenomenon. The city or agglomeration (megalopolis) then enters into an examination of the process of industrialization and urban space within the general space of development. In terms of Marxist terminology, the urban and the process of urbanization are simple superstructures of the mode of production (capitalist or socialist). It is often assumed that there is no interaction among urban phenomena, the relations of production, and productive forces. The reversal of perspective occurs when industrialization is considered to be a step toward urbanization, a moment, an intermediary, an instrument. In such a way that, within this twofold process (industrialization-urbanization), the second term becomes dominant following a period in which the first was dominant. From this point on, our concept of the "city" can no longer be limited to "optimizing" industrialization and its consequences, complaining about alienation in industrial society (whether through alienating individualism or overorganization), or wishing for a return to the urban communities of antiquity, whether Greek or medieval. These so-called models are only variations of urbanist ideology.

In this context, the *critique of everyday life* can play a surprising role. It is not merely a detail of sociology, an "object" that can be studied critically, or a "subject"; it has no clearly circumscribed domain. It makes use of economy and economic analysis, just as it does sociology, psychology, and linguistics. Yet it does not fall into any of those categories. And although it does not cover every aspect of praxis in the industrial era, it makes use of the most important results. That era resulted in the constitution of an *everydayness,* a social environment of sophisticated exploitation and carefully controlled passivity. Everydayness is not found within the "urban" as such but in and through generalized segregation: the segregation of moments of life and activities. The critical approach comprises the criticism of objects and subjects, sectors and domains. In showing how people live, the critique of everyday life builds an indictment of the strategies that lead to that result. Critical thought transgresses the boundaries separating the specialized sciences of human reality. It illuminates the practical uses of those sciences. It indicates the emergence and urgency of a new social practice no longer typical of "industrial" but of urban society. In this sense, the critique of everyday life (an ongoing critique, sometimes spontaneously self-critical, sometimes conceptually formulated) brings together the essential elements of the sociological study of the industrialized countries. By comparing the real and the possible (which is also "reality"), it draws conclusions, without, however, requiring an object or subject, a fixed system or domain. Given this orientation, we can even envisage urban sociology one day being given a definable status through the critique of needs and functionalities, structures, ideologies, and partial and reductive practices. The social practice that needs to be developed, that of urban society, has little immediate connection with what is currently referred to as urbanism.

As an ideology, urbanism dissimulates its strategies. The critique of urbanism is characterized by the need for a critique of urbanist ideologies and urbanist practices (as partial, that is, reductive, practices and class strategies). Such a critique can illuminate what is really happening in urban practice: the clumsy and unenlightened efforts to formulate and resolve some of the problems of urban society. For these strategies, which are dissimulated beneath the logic of class (the politics of space, economism, and so forth), it substitutes a strategy that is linked to the understanding.

Consideration of the urban phenomenon, by pushing philosophy to a new level and turning all the sciences to its own account through a form of radical critique, can define a *strategy*. Within this perspective, we can rationally define the limits and point of convergence, where apparently separate lines of thought come together.

This strategy appears in bifurcated form. However, the disjunction cannot mask a fundamental unity arising from the fact that full knowledge momentarily focused on a problematic becomes *political* in the strong sense of the term: the science of political (urban) reality. In a relative sense, the strategy devolves into a strategy of knowledge and a political strategy without any separation taking place.

Should the science of the urban phenomenon respond to pragmatic requirements, to immediate demands? Planners, programmers, and users want solutions. For what? To make people happy. To order them to be happy. It's a strange way of interpreting happiness. The science of the urban phenomenon cannot respond to these demands without the risk of validating external restrictions imposed by ideology and power. It constitutes itself slowly, making use of theoretical hypotheses and practical experience as well as established concepts. But it cannot exist without imagination, that is, without utopia. It must recognize that there are a multiplicity of situations. In some situations, demography dominates reality and, consequently, knowledge. This does not mean that demography will become dominant, but that it will have a voice, rather than the right or power to determine the future. In other situations, economics will dominate, helped by planners. But in doing so, economics lays itself open to a radical critique, which, although inconvenient for the field, is of undeniable utility and fecundity. Sociology and sociologists will also play a role in these developments. It is possible that research on cities and the urban phenomenon would enable us to construct macrosociological models. During this process (strategically oriented), sociology in general and urban sociology, led to reconsider their categories and concepts, may be able to generate a body of scientific knowledge centered on the problematic. Within an industrial framework, however, these "disciplines" can do no more than oscillate between the role of servants of (private or public) interests and the discourse between contestant and contested. In any event, and regardless of the outcome, the means can never be substituted for the end, or the part for the whole, or tactics for strategy. Any tactic associated with a given specialization will be severely criticized as soon as it attempts to become strategy on a global level: imperialism.

The strategy of knowledge cannot be isolated. It strives toward practice; in other words, the incessant confrontation with experience and the constitution of a coherent global practice, that of urban society (the practice of adopting time and space to the human being, a superior modality of freedom).

However, until the new order, social practice will belong to politicians, who will control it through institutions and systems. More specifically, specialist politicians, like specialists themselves, will block the formation of a higher rationality, that of urban democracy. They operate within the very institutional and ideological frameworks that need to be overcome. This complicates the situation considerably. The strategy of knowledge is doubly constricted. Because it cannot avoid an awareness of political strategies, it must familiarize itself with them. How can it avoid having knowledge of those objects and subjects, systems and domains? Political sociology and the institutional analysis of administrations and bureaucracies have a large role to play in this. Strategic activities can include proposals to politicians, government officials, factions, and parties. This does not mean that critical knowledge should step down and give way to these specialist politicians. Quite the contrary. How can we provide them with projects and programs without abandoning a critical analysis of their ideologies and realizations? How can we persuade or constrain them if we respond to their pressure with an opposing pressure? Although the solution is far from simple, it would be fatal if knowledge were to abandon its right to criticize decisions and institutions. Every failure would trigger a process that would be difficult to reverse. And here, it is democracy that steps down and not just science and scientific institutions.

Strategy contains a key element: the optimal and maximal use of technology (all technologies) for solving urban questions to improve everyday life in urban society. This exposes the possibility of transforming everyday life as we understand it through the rational use of machinery and technology (which also includes the transformation of social relationships). The co-optation of initiatives (of every initiative) in the order of existing things by a "system" of some kind does not mean that such proposals cannot be used to clear and highlight a path. Economic forecasts and state power rarely envisage the optimal use of resources, technology, or scientific tools based on a body of contemporary experience. They are used only when under pressure from opinion, emergency, or direct challenge (assuming it can be exercised). This is the result of budgetary and financial, that is, "economic," requirements. These requirements mask other, less obvious motives. Powers have their own strategy, systems their own interests, which all too often relegate such important issues to the background.

The reliance on philosophy in no way implies a nostalgia for the past. Here, the distinction between philosophic thought and metaphilosophy assumes meaning and importance. Metaphilosophy is the new context in which theories and concepts, signifying units detached from their philosophical context, assume a different meaning. To get a clearer idea of the scope of the current problematic, that is to say, actuality as problematic, we can make use of philosophical thought—with the understanding that we are making a transition from classical philosophy to metaphilosophy.

What about totality? Dialectically speaking, it is present, here and now. It is absent as well. In every human act and possibly in the natural world as well, all moments are contained: work and play, knowledge and repose, effort and enjoyment, joy and sorrow. But these moments need to be "objectivized" in reality and society; they also require a form for their elaboration. Although close by in this sense, totality is also distant: lived immediacy and horizon. Urban society transcends the opposition between nature and culture created by the ideology of the industrial era. It puts an end to the things that make totality impossible: unresolvable division, absolute separation, programmed segregation. However, it only provides us with a *path*, not a model of totality. This was the method of conventional philosophy, but not metaphilosophy, for which path and model are contrasting oppositions.

The development of an urban strategy can only proceed using general rules of political analysis, which have been around since Marx. This analysis covers conditions and cycles as well as the structural elements of a situation. How and when should we separate specifically urban objectives from those associated with industrial production, planning, the distribution of revenue (surplus value), employment, the organization of the enterprise and labor? The most serious error would be the premature separation of objectives. In fact, the industrial revolution and the urban revolution are two aspects of a radical transformation of the world. They are two elements (dialectically united) of the same process, a single idea, that of global revolution. While it is true that the second aspect has increased in importance so that it is no longer subordinate to the first, this does not imply that the first suddenly ceases to have any importance or reality. Political analysis of a situation has no bearing on the "real," in the trivial and most frequently used sense of the term, but on the dialectical relationship of the three terms: the real, the possible, and the impossible, so as to make possible what appeared to be impossible. Any analysis that approaches the real must accept political opportunism. Any analysis that diverges and moves too close to the impossible (toward the utopic in the banal sense of the term) is doomed to failure.

It is a recognized fact that the Americas have entered a phase of urban guerrilla activity. The technological advance in North America and its influence on Latin America (including Mexico) have made this a privileged continent in a way, at least from the point of view I am concerned with here. Just as Marx based his analysis on England and English capitalism, the political analyses of the urban transformation are based on a detailed study of North and South America. Urban guerrilla activity doesn't have the same characteristics in North America and Latin America. Blacks in the United States, who are locked in urban ghettos by a form of social segregation that is more powerful than legal integration, have resorted to desperate acts. Many of those blacks, many young people in general, have rejected any political program, and consider the search for such a program to be a form of treason. They want to unleash violence in its pure state. Until now there has been no direct relation between violent acts and the urban crisis to which American society has fallen prey. That society did not experience any fundamental crisis during the industrial period. It attempted—and it continues—to organize itself around the rationality of business, while retaining forms (ideological, political, urban) that antedate industrial growth. Within the overall context, the relations between local authorities, the federal government, and the states have become increasingly complicated. The largest cities (New York is typical) have become uncontrol-lable, ungovernable, a knot of problems that are increasingly difficult to resolve. It is obvious that for strategy to succeed it must combine the "negative" forces of revolt against a repres-sive society with social forces that are capable of "positively" resolving the problems of the megalopolis. This is no simple matter. Just because this society has entered a phase of urban revolution does not mean that the urban problematic can be easily resolved. It simply means that a highly industrialized society, if it fails to respond to the urban problematic by a transformation capable of resolving it, will collapse into a form of chaos that is masked by an ideology of order and satisfaction. Yet the difficulty of theoretical analysis and the discovery of solutions shouldn't discourage either thought or action. A similar situation occurred at the beginning of the twentieth century with the industrial problematic. The second half of this century may call into question Marx's optimistic comment that humanity presents itself only with problems it can resolve, but it is still too early to deliberately abandon this belief. Optimism has one thing in its favor—its tenacity.

In South America, urban guerrilla activity is taking place in the favelas, or shantytowns, which have become outlets for struggle, intermediaries between the dispossessed peas-ants and industrial labor. In all likelihood, Che Guevara committed an error. His attempt to create centers of peas-ant guerrilla activity came too late. A few years earlier, in Cuba, there was still a possibility that this might have suc-ceeded. The South American countryside was emptied of its population; the best of the peasants emigrated en masse to the outskirts of the already overcrowded cities. As of this writing, the objectives of urban guerrilla activity do not ap-pear to have been very well defined (at least until additional information is available).

What about Asia? Has Asia concluded the period of

agrarian and industrial transformation? The existence of large cities is an inadequate marker. It is the totality of their relations with the countryside that needs to be examined. The concept of unequal development may be useful here for an analysis that does not coincide with the work of Lenin but expands on it. The enormous numbers of peasants, the latent or violent pressure, questions of agrarian reform and industrialization—all continue to mask the urban problematic. This situation helps explain the theory according to which the "global city," incapable of transformative actions, will fall victim to the "global struggle."

With respect to the socialist countries, there are three possibilities: First, the urban problematic, stifled by the ideology of industrial production, will fail to enter people's consciousness. An official urbanism, not very dissimilar from capitalist urbanism (except that there is less emphasis on the centrality of exchange and greater access to the soil and, therefore, an increase in the amount of green space, the zero degree of urban reality), will continue to pass for a solution that realizes socialist society. Second, the pressure of urban reality will burst the ideology of productivist socialism and expose the absurdity of a state philosophy that claims that production and productive labor possess a meaning and finality no longer based on profit. It will raise awareness of an active criticism of state socialism as well as the fusion between civil society and political society, to the benefit of the latter. In this way urban society will reshape civil society and lead to the absorption of political society into civil society (Marx's withering away of the state). Third, a strategic hypothesis: legal bodies and institutions will grow increasingly aware of the urban problematic; the transformation will take place gradually through legal means.

There is no need to choose among these three strategies, especially since we don't have the information to do so. The only ones authorized to choose are those willing to take the risks and assume the responsibilities. Here, my intention is simply to outline the possibilities, point out a path, and distinguish among the various strategies.

In France, the moment may yet arrive when urban objectives diverge from (without actually separating from) specifically industrial objectives. This would involve either the formation of a new political party or an effort to involve an existing party in the politicization of urban issues. In this sense, could the "crisis of the left" be explained by its inability to analyze these issues or the fact that it has framed them so narrowly? The urban problem has ceased to be a municipal problem and has become national and global. The reduction of the urban to housing and infrastructure is part of the shortsightedness of political life on the right as well as the left. The most important political truth that the French "left" (what remains of it) must understand if it is to remain viable is the existence of a vast urban program, which would also be a project for the transformation of the everyday, and which would have no further relationship either with a repressive and banal urbanism or with the limitations of national development programs.

Could Les Halles serve as a salutary example of what might happen elsewhere in France? If so, that would be very unfortunate. In actuality, the fate of the center of Paris had been decided over a century ago: Haussmann's urbanism and the failure of the Commune sealed its fate. This center, the area surrounding Les Halles, has again shown a surprising lack of segregation. Every category of the population was represented (similar to the national averages: artisans, merchants, laborers, professionals). This contrasted strangely with the segregation visible in the neighboring ghetto (Rue des Rosiers and the surrounding area). However, the number of artisans and small shops began to dwindle. A return to the center of a moneyed class, sickened by the suburbs, just as they were by traditional bourgeois neighborhoods—in simple terms, the elitist gentrification of an urban center cut off from production—has been going on for years. Only the most recent arrivals, self-employed professionals for the most part (film, theater, couture, the arts), have been able to "modernize" the houses in these neighborhoods, which were formerly the reserve of the bourgeoisie and subsequently abandoned by them (as in the Marais).[2] Although these neighborhoods were considered to be "active" and "picturesque," a large percentage of this mixed population lived in slum dwellings. So what happened? The leaders and members of the various committees opposed to speculative activities, opposed to the asphyxiation of central Paris, opposed to the deportation of the poorest tenants, were people whose existence was not threatened by the activities taking place. And what about those people? What were they waiting for? Better housing, better jobs, or simply jobs. The other groups represented so-called private interests; they were capable of various activities but incapable of forceful political action. Aside from the engineering aspect, which was technically questionable, the attitudes of the participants were clearly drawn: those in power wanted to build an enormous finance ministry in the center of Paris, which would become a hub for government decisions. The so-called communist opposition wanted to see inexpensive residential quarters built on the site. Two mediocrities, squared off against one another, one bureaucratic, the other electoral.

The strategy of knowledge implies (1) a radical critique of what is called urbanism, its ambiguity, its contradictions, its variants, what it avows and what it hides; (2) the development of a science of the urban phenomenon, beginning with its form and content (aiming at convergence through the unity of these two approaches).

Political strategy implies the following:

1. The introduction of the urban problematic into (French) political life by moving it to the foreground.
2. The development of a program that begins with a form of generalized self-management. The self-management introduced in industry—not without some difficulty—can "trigger" urban self-management. But this can also move into the foreground and in turn trigger the practice of self-management in industry. Yet both urban life and industry require more than self-management. On its own, looking at each isolated unit, it is doomed to failure. The problems of urban self-management are related to those of industrial self-management but far more wide-ranging, for they also involve markets and the control of investments—that is, an overall program.
3. The introduction into the enlarged, transformed, concretized contractual system of a "right to the city" (the right not to be excluded from centrality and its movement).

8 || The Urban Illusion

[handwritten margin note: objective definition of urbanism. physical trace on the land of human dwellings of stone, cement, or metal]

We can now provide an *objective* definition of urbanism, which is officially defined as the "physical trace on the land of human dwellings of stone, cement, or metal." We now have the conceptual tools for a radical critique of an activity that claims to control the process of urbanization and urban practice and subject it to its order. Our perception of this activity differs from the way it perceives itself: simultaneously art and science, technology and understanding. This unitary character is illusory, however. In fact, urbanism, when examined closely, breaks into pieces. There are several urbanisms: the urbanism of humanists, of developers, of the state and its technocrats. The first group proposes abstract utopias; the second sells urbanism—that is, happiness, a lifestyle, a certain social standing. The activity of the last group dissociates, like the activity of the state, into will and representation, institutions and ideologies. The simultaneous pressures from these two aspects of state urbanism in no way provide the unitary and coherently ordered character it claims to possess. Some might retort, "Without urbanists, there would be chaos." It is chaos, but one that is the result of an imposed order. Lacking an appropriate methodology (dialectic), urbanist theory has been unable to comprehend the twofold process of urbanization and industrialization, one that is characterized by its extreme complexity and conflict. It can hardly be claimed as an asset that urbanists perceive—from afar—the sense of urgency and the problems associated with the new scarcity of space, time, place, and natural "elements."

The urban illusion can't be separated from other illusions, which should also be denounced, using the same strategy of knowledge. There is nothing especially negative about the term "illusion." It is not a form of personal insult or an ad hominem argument against anyone in particular. Those who interpret it that way are simply suffering the pangs of a bad conscience. Is there anyone who is free of all illusion? The most tenacious, the most effective illusions are the illusions of class, whose origins are both higher and more distant than intellectual or individual errors. Their course passes well over the heads of those they most affect.

The philosophical illusion arises from the belief on the part of philosophers that they can enclose the world in a system of their own devising. They assume that their system is based on precedent, since it includes everything and is hermetically enclosed. Yet there is always more in the world than in any philosophical system. Philosophical activity wasn't only honorable. For years it rivaled art, possessing something of the incomparable character of an oeuvre: something unique, infinitely precious, irreplaceable. Isn't it an illusion, then, to go on indefinitely building systems that are forever disappointing, always improved? From the moment the idea of the indefinite perfectibility of systemization comes into conflict with the idea of the immanent perfection of the system as such, philosophical illusion enters consciousness.

The state illusion is part of a colossal and ludicrous project. The state is capable of managing the affairs of tens of millions of subjects. It would like to direct our consciousness

state *illusion*

as if it were a kind of high-level administrator. Providential, a god personified, the state would become the center of things and conscious beings on earth. One might assume that such an illusion would crumble as soon as it was formulated. But this is not the case. It seems inherent in the projects and ambitions of those who want to be, and claim to be, elected officials, high- or low-level administrators, political leaders. The very idea of the state implies this project, which is acknowledged only in secret. Once the project is discredited, once it is abandoned by thought and will, the state begins to decline.

The urban illusion is closely related to the two illusions discussed above. Like classical philosophy, urbanism claims to be a system. It pretends to embrace, enclose, possess a new totality. It wants to be the modern philosophy of the city, justified by (liberal) humanism while justifying a (technocratic) utopia.

In the case of ideology, neither good will nor good intentions are justifications. In fact, a clear conscience and peace of mind merely aggravate the situation. How can we define the fundamental void in urbanism, whether the product of private intellect or public institutions? To the extent that it claims to replace or supplant urban practice it fails to examine that practice. But for urbanists, this practice is precisely the blind field I discussed earlier. They live it, they are in it, but they don't see it, and certainly cannot grasp it as such. With complete peace of mind, they substitute its representations of space, of social life, of groups and their relationships for praxis. They don't know where these representations come from or what they imply—that is, the logic and strategy that they serve. And if they do know, their knowledge is unforgivable; their ideological cover splits to reveal a strange nudity.

In bureaucratic capitalism, productive activity completely escapes the control of planners and developers. Technicians and technocrats are asked for their advice. People sit around listening politely—most of the time, at least. But they are not the decision makers. In spite of their efforts, they cannot escape the status that has been given to them, that of a pressure group or caste, and they become a class. The same holds true for the so-called socialist countries. But for their technocrats, space is the site of their future exploits, the terrain of their victories, so to speak. Space is available. Why? Because it is almost empty or seems to be. Corporations, productive units, and established networks are dispersed in space but do not fill it. Free space belongs to thought, to action. Technocratic thought oscillates between the representation of empty space, nearly geometric, occupied only by concepts, by the most rational logics and strategies, and the representation of a permeated space, occupied by the results of those logics and strategies. They fail to perceive that every space is a *product* and that this product does not arise in conceptual thought, which is not necessarily immediately productive. Space, as product, results from relationships of production that are taken control of by an active group. Urbanists seem to be unaware of or misinterpret the fact that they themselves figure in these relationships of production as organizers and administrators. They implement, they do not control, space. They obey a social command that is not directed at any given object or any given product (commodity) but a global object, the supreme product, the ultimate object of exchange: space. The deployment of the world of commodities now affects not only objects but their containers, it is no longer limited to content, to objects in space. More recently, space itself has begun to be bought and sold. Not the earth, the soil, but *social space,* produced as such, with this purpose, this finality (so to speak). Space is no longer only an indifferent medium, the sum of places where surplus value is created, realized, and distributed. It becomes the product of social labor, the very general object of production, and consequently of the formation of surplus value. This is how production becomes social within the very framework of neocapitalism. In the recent past this would have been unforeseen and unforeseeable, since production and the social nature of production were thought of only in terms of the enterprise and the productive labor of the enterprise. Today the social (global) nature of productive labor, embodied in productive forces, is apparent in the social production of space. In the recent past, there was no other way to conceive of "production" other than as an object, located somewhere in space: an ordinary object, a machine, a book, a painting. Today, space as a whole enters into production as a product, through the buying, selling, and exchange of parts of space. Not too long ago, a localized, identifiable space, the soil, still belonged to a sacred entity: the earth. It belonged to that cursed, and therefore sacred, character, the owner (not of the means of production, but of the Home), a carryover from feudal times. Today, this ideology and the corresponding practice are collapsing. Something new is happening.

The production of space is not new in itself. Dominant groups have always produced a particular space, the space of the old cities, of the countryside (and what will become the "natural" landscape). What is new is the global and total production of social space. This enormous expansion of productive activity is carried out on behalf of those who invented it, manage it, and profit from it. Capitalism appears to be out of steam. It found new inspiration in the conquest of space—in trivial terms, in real estate speculation, capital projects (inside and outside the city), the buying and selling of space. And it did so on a worldwide scale. This is the (unforeseen) path of the socialization of productive forces, of the production of space itself. Capitalism, to ensure its survival, took the initiative in this. The strategy goes far beyond simply selling space, bit by bit. Not only does it incorporate space in the production of surplus value, it attempts to completely reorganize production as something subordinate to the centers of information and decision making.

Urbanism encompasses this enormous operation, dissimulating its fundamental features, meanings, and finality. Beneath its benign exterior, humanist and technological, it masks capitalist strategy: the control of space, the struggle against the trend toward lower profits, and so on.

This strategy overwhelms the "user," the "participant," the simple "inhabitant." He is reduced not only to merely functioning as an inhabitant (habitat as function) but to being a buyer of space, one who realizes surplus value. Space becomes a place where various functions are carried out, the most important and most hidden being that of forming, realizing, and distributing in novel ways the surplus of an entire society (generalized surplus value within the capitalist mode of production).

Urban ideology exaggerates the importance of the so-called planned activities it sanctions. It gives the impression, to those who use these representations, of managing people and things in innovative and positive ways. With considerable naïveté (genuine or otherwise), many people believe they are determining and creating social life and social relations (human). Here the urban illusion awakens the somewhat somnolent mythology of the Architect. In the new ideology the old myths agree with and support one another. The result is a series of (occasionally cancerous) growths that are grafted onto real knowledge and concrete practice (that of users who are still attached to use value).

Ideology and its application (by the corresponding institutions) overwhelm actual practice. Use (use value), which had been pushed aside with the development of exchange value (the world of commodities, its logic and language, its system of signs and significations clinging to each object), continues to be overwhelmed by urban representations, by the encouragement and motivation so freely assigned to it. Practice disappears; it falls silent, becomes passive. A surprising paradox arises from this: the passivity of vested interests.

There are many reasons for this. Here I'll examine one of them, certainly not the least important: urban ideology as *reductive* of practice (of habiting, of urban reality). As with any ideology, it does not stop at being simply reductive. It systematically extrapolates and concludes, as if it held and manipulated all the elements of the question, as if it had resolved the urban problematic in and through a total theory, one that was immediately applicable.

This extrapolation becomes excessive when it tends toward a kind of medical ideology. The urbanist imagines himself caring for and healing a sick society, a pathological space. He perceives spatial diseases, which are initially conceived abstractly as an available void, then fragmented into partial contents. Eventually, space itself becomes a subject. It suffers, grows ill, must be taken care of so it can be returned to (moral) health. The urban illusion culminates in delirium. Space, and the thought of space, lead the thinker down a dangerous path. He becomes schizophrenic and imagines a mental illness—the schizophrenia of society—onto which he projects his own illness, space sickness, mental vertigo.

If we look at the various urbanist proposals, we find that they don't go very far. They are limited to cutting space into grids and squares. Technocrats, unaware of what goes on in their own mind and in their working concepts, profoundly misjudging what is going on (and what is not) in their blind field, end up minutely organizing a repressive space. For all that, they have a clear conscience. They are unaware that space harbors an ideology (more exactly, an *ideo-logic*). They are unaware, or pretend to be unaware, that urbanism, objective in appearance (because it is a function of the state and dependent on skills and knowledge), is a form of class urbanism and incorporates a class strategy (a particular logic). In this domain, is "technostructure" as effective (in maintaining the relationships of production that exist, ensuring their survival and development) as it is within the enterprise? There is cause to wonder. For isn't it precisely in this sector that technostructure and the "compensatory power" of great economic and political power structures (Galbraith) reach their "optimal" efficiency? They manage this by allowing logic and strategy to conceal themselves from view—and strategy to appear logical, or necessary.

As it exists in the current framework, that is, as a functional entity (although this is not and possibly cannot be acknowledged), urbanism has been unable to escape the permanent crisis described above and remains stigmatized; it is unable to find a status for itself, nor is the urbanist able to find a role. Urbanism finds itself caught between particular interests and political interests, between those who decide on behalf of "private" interests and those who decide on behalf of higher institutions and powers. It lives off the compromise between neoliberalism (which participates in planning and in activities that are referred to as "voluntary" or "consensual") and neo-dirigisme (which leaves a field of action open for "free enterprise"). The urbanist slips into the crack between them, into the fissure between developers and power structures. The ideal situation for the urbanist is the (unconscious) conflict between representation and will, and this includes elected officials. Urban reality and its problematic break apart in the face of theory and in practice into scattered representations ("environment," "infrastructure") and skills (consulting firms, offices, institutions). Urbanism and the urbanist can only accept this fragmentation; indeed, they contribute to it. Whenever they act, it is always in an "official" capacity. At the same time, urbanism claims to be a doctrine. It tends toward unity: theory, logic, strategy. But when a unitary function reveals itself and becomes effective, that unity is lost. It is the strategy of profit or the logic of industrial space, the logic of exchange and the world of commodities, or . . .

As a form of representation, urbanism is nothing more

than an ideology that claims to be either "art" or "technology" or "science," depending on the context. This ideology pretends to be straightforward, yet it obfuscates, harbors things unsaid: which it covers, which it contains, as a form of will tending toward efficiency. Urbanism is doubly fetishistic. First, it implies the fetishism of satisfaction. What about vested interests? They must be satisfied, and therefore their needs must be understood and catered to, unchanged. From time to time, these needs can be modified. The implicit assumption is that we can determine those needs, either because those vested interests have openly stated them or because experts have studied them. We can classify them. For each need, an object is supplied. This assumption is inherently false, especially since it neglects to take into consideration *social needs*. Second, it implies the fetishism of space. Space is creation. Whoever creates space creates whatever it is that fills space. The place engenders the thing and the good place engenders good things. Which results in ambiguity, misunderstanding, a singular oscillation.

Either the disease of space excuses people but acknowledges skills, or the disease of people in a good space is inexcusable. The fetishism of space is not without its contradictions, for it fails to resolve the conflict between use and exchange, even when it crushes both use and user.

Rather than analyzing the contradictions of space, I would like to highlight the role played by urbanism and more generally real estate (speculation, construction) in neocapitalist society. Real estate functions as a second sector, a circuit that runs parallel to that of industrial production, which serves the nondurable assets market, or at least those that are less durable than buildings. This second sector serves as a buffer. It is where capital flows in the event of a depression, although enormous profits soon slow to a trickle. In this sector, there are few "multipliers," few spin-offs. Capital is tied up in real estate. Although the overall economy (so-called domestic economy) soon begins to suffer, the role and function of this sector continue to grow. As the principal circuit—current industrial production and the movable property that results—begins to slow down, capital shifts to the second sector, real estate. It can even happen that real-estate speculation becomes the principal source for the formation of capital, that is, the realization of surplus value. As the percentage of overall surplus value formed and realized by industry begins to decline, the percentage created and realized by real-estate speculation and construction increases. The second circuit supplants the first, becomes essential. But as economists are accustomed to saying, this is an unhealthy situation. The role played by real estate in various countries (especially Spain and Greece) continues to be poorly understood, poorly situated within the general mechanisms of capitalist economy. It is a source of problems. It is here that the "compensatory power" discussed earlier can come into play. However, urbanism as an ideology and as an institution (as representation and will) masks these problems. It seems to contain a response and therefore seems to preclude the need for their theoretical investigation. Because urbanism is situated at the intersection of these two sectors (the production of movable goods and the production of real estate), it conceals that intersection.

Urbanism is, although unwittingly, class urbanism. When the urbanist realizes this, when he attains this level of knowledge, he becomes cynical or simply resigns. As a cynic, he may even sell freedom, happiness, lifestyles, social life, even community life, in phalansteries designed for the use of modern satraps.

Urbanism is therefore subject to radical critique. It masks a situation. It conceals operations. It blocks a view of the horizon, a path to urban knowledge and practice. It accompanies the decline of the spontaneous city and the historical urban core. It implies the intervention of power more than that of understanding. Its only coherence, its only logic, is that of the state—the void. The state can only separate, disperse, hollow out vast voids, the squares and avenues built in its own image—an image of force and constraint.

Urbanism prevents thought from becoming a consideration of the possible, a reflection of the future. It encloses thought in a situation where three terms—critical thought, reformist ideology, leftist opposition—clash, a situation from which thought must escape, a situation from which urbanism and the urbanist prevent it from escaping.

Yet not everything about urbanism is negative. More specifically, it is nothing more than the opposition between the "blinding and the blinded," to the extent that the urbanist believes himself to be someone capable of broad ideas, interdisciplinary, a creator of space and human relationships. Moreover, the urbanist amasses data and information. Urbanism provides a presentiment of new scarcities and occasionally the opportunity to explore them: space, time, desire, the elements (water, air, earth, the sun). Of course, urbanists tend to avoid the concrete and fundamental question of the (social) management of scarcities that replace older scarcities (in the so-called advanced countries). The urbanist often perceives the importance of the question man asks of "nature" and nature of man. His reading of space encourages him to read nature—that is, to contemplate the rape and destruction of that nature. In fact, couldn't some of Le Corbusier's texts be read in this sense, "symptomatically" (rather than literally)? Or some of the so-called urbanist works, less well known but significant for the ideology they transmit? Urbanist discourses are sometimes articulated using the discourse of urban practice. A deformed image of the future and the possible may still contain their traces and indexes. The utopian part of urbanist projects (generally masked by technology and the abuse of technicism) is not without interest as a precursor symptom, which signals a problematic without explaining it. This does not mean that there exists an epistemology of urbanism, a theoretical core that can virtually generate an urban practice. Far from it. In fact, the argument I have developed would claim the contrary. For the moment, for a long time into the future, the problematic will outweigh our understanding. What is most needed is that we categorize, that we prepare concepts (categories) we can verify, that we explore the possible-impossible, and that we do so through transduction.

The question comes to mind of whether urbanism today doesn't play the role ideology (philosophy + political economy + utopian socialism) did around 1845, when Marxist and critical (revolutionary) thought concerning industrial phenomena were being formed. This seemingly harsh interpretation contains an element of exaggerated praise. Do doctrinaire urbanists possess the scope that Hegel, Fourier, Saint-Simon, Adam Smith, or Ricardo had? Even if we were to compare them to minor ideologues like Bauer and Stirner rather than the great theorists, we would still be aiming too high.[1] Urbanism could be more accurately compared to common political economy than to Marxist economic analysis. For these economists, the critical point of view holds little interest. Sometimes, they say the same things as the Marxists in a different language. Rostow, for example, calls "takeoff" what the Marxists refer to as "primitive accumulation."[2] Their schemas frequently contain a tactical element, which they refer to as "operational." The characteristics of this tactic are easily discernible through analysis or application. More often, the abstract models used by economists are put safely to rest in drawers. Business executives and politicians do as they please. Couldn't the same be said about our urbanists?

Still, urbanism remains an impediment because of its *models*. Once again, this reflects one of the inherent conflicts in contemporary political and scientific thought, the conflict between *path* and *model.* To clear a path, we have to destroy the models.

Given the confusion surrounding ideology, it is worth repeating that my criticism of urbanism is a criticism of the left (by the left). Right-wing criticism, whether liberal or neoliberal, attacks urbanism as an institution but extols the initiatives of developers. This leaves the path open for capitalist developers, who are now able to invest profitably in the real-estate sector; the era of urban illusion has given them an opportunity to adapt. The radical critique of urban illusion opens the way to urban practice and the theory associated with this practice, which will advance together during the process of overall *development* (if this development assumes greater importance than growth, together with its ideologies and strategies).

This "leftist" critique involves much more than a rejection of liberalism or neoliberalism by challenging private enterprise and the state, individual initiative and political paternalism. Such a critique can only become radical by rejecting the state, the role of the state, the strategy of the state, and the politics of space. It does so by demonstrating that the *promotion of the urban* is tied to the rejection of economic (quantitative) growth seen as an end in itself, the orientation of production for other purposes, the primacy of (qualitative) development over growth, the limitation of the state (the quintessential limiter) to a subordinate function—in short, a radical critique of the state and politics.

The worst utopia is the one that remains unnamed. The urban illusion belongs to the state. It is a state utopia: a cloud on the mountain that blocks the road. It is both antitheory and antipractice.

What is urbanism? A superstructure of neocapitalist society, a form of "organizational capitalism," which is not the same as "organized capital"—in other words, a *bureaucratic*

society of controlled consumption. Urbanism organizes a sector that appears to be free and accessible, open to rational activity: inhabited space. It controls the consumption of space and the habitat. As superstructure, it must be distinguished from practice, from social relationships, from society itself. There has been some confusion between urbanism and the "urban," namely urban practice and the urban phenomenon. This confusion would explain the pseudo-Marxist theory, apparently vigorously critiqued, that claims that the urban phenomenon is itself only a superstructure. These ideologies confuse practice with ideology, social with institutional relations. It is only from an ideological and institutional point of view, however, that urbanism reveals to critical analysis the illusions that it harbors and that foster its implementation. In this light, urbanism appears as the vehicle for a limited and tendentious rationality in which space, deceptively neutral and apolitical, constitutes an object (objective).

[handwritten annotation: urbanism organizes a sector appearing to be free & accessible = inhabited space]

9 || Urban Society

The concept developed earlier as a (scientific) hypothesis can now be approached differently. I hope that readers will have a better understanding of it now that it has been freed somewhat of its earlier theoretical status. However, the process is far from complete, and it would be dogmatic to claim that it was. To do so would mean inserting the concept of an "urban society" into a questionable epistemology that we should be wary of because it is premature, because it places the categorical above the problematic, thereby halting, and possibly shifting, the very movement that brought the urban phenomenon to the threshold of awareness in the first place.

The concept of an urban society has freed itself from the myths and ideologies that bind it, whether they arise in the agrarian stages of history and consciousness or in an unwarranted extension of the representations borrowed from the corporate sphere (industrial rationalism). Myths become a part of literature; their poetic and utopian character in no way diminishes their attraction. We also know that ideology has played a large part in the development of a body of doctrine known as urbanism. To continue our exploration of the blind field, we had to jettison that opaque, heavy body: the urban phenomenon in its totality.

The unconscious (the boundary between the misunderstood and the one who misunderstands) appears sometimes as a deceptive and blinding emergence of a rural and industrial past, sometimes as a sense of loss for an urban reality that is slipping away.

In this way, the notion of a critical zone or phase comes into view. Within this zone, the terrain flies before us, the ground is booby-trapped. Although the old concepts no longer work, new concepts are beginning to take shape. Reality isn't the only thing to go; thought itself begins to give way.

Still, we have succeeded in elaborating a coherent discourse that is nonideological and that is both *of* the urban (inside an emergent urban universe) and *about* the urban (describing it, outlining its contours). This kind of discourse can never be completed. Its incompletion is an essential part of its existence. It is defined as a reflection of the future, implying operations in time as well as space: transduction (construction of a virtual object) and the exploration of the possible-impossible. The temporal dimension, evacuated by epistemology and the philosophy of knowledge, is victoriously reintroduced. Yet transduction is not long-range planning. Like urbanism, it has been called into question; like urbanism it contains a strategy. It mixes ideology and scientificity. Here, as elsewhere, scientificity is an ideology, an excrescence grafted onto real, but fragmentary, knowledge. And like urbanism, long-range planning also extrapolates from a reductive position.

During this exploration, the urban phenomenon appears as something other than, as something more than, a superstructure (of the mode of production). I say this in response to a form of Marxist dogmatism that manifests itself in a variety of ways. The urban problematic is worldwide. The same problems are found in socialism and in capitalism—

along with the failure to respond. Urban society can only be defined as global. Virtually, it covers the planet by recreating nature, which has been wiped out by the industrial exploitation of natural resources (material and "human"), by the destruction of so-called natural particularities.

Moreover, the urban phenomenon has had a profound effect on the methods of production: productive forces, relationships of production, and the contradictions between them. It both extends and accentuates, on a new plane, the social character of productive labor and its conflict with the ownership (private) of the means of production. It continues the "socialization of society," which is another way of saying that the urban does not eliminate industrial contradictions. It does not resolve them for the sole reason that it has become dominant. What's more, the conflicts inherent in production (in the relationships of production and capitalist ownership as well as in "socialist" society) hinder the urban phenomenon, prevent urban development, reducing it to growth. This is particularly true of the action of the state under capitalism and state socialism.

To summarize then: Society becomes increasingly complex with the transition from the rural to the industrial and from the industrial to the urban. This multifaceted complexification affects space as well as time, for the complexification of space and the objects that occupy space cannot occur without a complexification of time and the activities that occur over time.

This space is occupied by interrelated networks, relationships that are defined by interference. Its homogeneity corresponds to intentions, unified strategies, and systematized logics, on the one hand, and reductive, and consequently simplifying, representations, on the other. At the same time, differences become more pronounced in populating this space, which tends, like any abstract space, toward homogeneity (quantitative, geometric, and logical space). This, in turn, results in conflict and a strange sense of unease. For this space tends toward a unique code, an absolute system, that of exchange and exchange value, of the logical thing and the logic of things. At the same time, it is filled with subsystems, partial codes, messages, and signifiers that do not become part of the unitary procedure that the space stipulates, prescribes, and inscribes in various ways.

The thesis of complexification appears philosophical. And sometimes it is, at least for certain authors (Teilhard de Chardin, for example). Here it is related to a fragmentary but effective scientific understanding: theories of information, message theories, encoding and decoding. We can, therefore, again state that this thesis is *metaphilosophical*—simultaneously global and articulated through the understanding.

The concept of complexification continues to be of service. It is theoretically based on the distinction between growth and development, a distinction imposed by the period, by experience, by a consideration of results. Marx distinguished growth and development only because he wanted to avoid any confusion between quantity and quality. But for Marx the growth (quantitative) and development (qualitative) of society could and must occur simultaneously. Unfortunately, history shows that this is not the case. Growth can occur without development and sometimes development can occur without growth. For half a century, growth has been at work just about everywhere, while rigid social and political relations have been maintained. Although the Soviet Union underwent a period of intense development between 1920 and 1935, objective "factors," namely the productive forces that were left behind by this "superstructure" explosion and the growth targets used as strategic objectives—means construed as ends—soon took their revenge. Wasn't the same true of France after the explosion of May 1968? The law of unequal development (Lenin) should be extended, expanded, and formulated in such a way that it can account for the conflict between growth and development that was revealed during the course of the twentieth century.

The theory of complexification anticipates the revenge of development over growth. The same is true for the theory of urban society. This revenge is only just beginning. The basic proposition, that growth cannot continue indefinitely and that the means can remain an end without a catastrophe occurring, still seems paradoxical.

These considerations evoke the prodigious extension of the urban to the entire planet, that is, urban society, its virtualities and potential. It goes without saying that this extension-expansion is not going to be problem-free. Indeed, it has been shown that the urban phenomenon tends to overflow borders, while commercial exchange and industrial and financial organizations, which once seemed to abolish those territorial limits (through the global market, through multinationals), now appear to reaffirm them. In any event, the effects of a possible rupture in industry and finance (a crisis of overproduction, a monetary crisis) would be accentuated by an extension of the urban phenomenon and the formation of urban society.

I have already introduced the idea of the "global city," generally attributed to Maoism, if not Mao Tse-tung himself. I would now like to develop this idea. The global city extends the traditional concept and image of the city to a global scale: a political center for the administration, protection, and operation of a vast territory. This is appropriate for the oriental city within the framework of an Asian mode of production. However, urban society cannot be constructed on the ruins of the classical city alone. In the West, this city has already begun to fragment. This fragmentation (explosion-implosion) may appear to be a precursor of urban society. It is part of its problematic and the critical phase that precedes it. However, a known strategy, which specifically makes use of urbanism, tends to view the political city as a decision-making center. Such a center is obviously not limited to collecting information upstream and distributing it downstream. It is not just a center of abstract decision making but a center of power. Yet power requires wealth, and vice versa. That is, the decision-making center, in the strategy being analyzed here, will serve as a point of attachment to the soil for a hyperorganized and rigidly systematized state. Formerly, the entire metropolitan land area played a central role with respect to the colonies and semicolonies, sucking up wealth, imposing its own order. Today, domination is consolidated in a physical locale, a capital (or a decision-making center that does not necessarily coincide with the capital). As a result, control is exercised throughout the national territory, which is transformed into a semicolony.

Part of my analysis may appear at first glance to correspond to the so-called Maoist interpretation of the "global city," but this interpretation raises a number of objections. There is nothing that prevents emerging centers of power from encountering obstacles and failing. What's more, any contradictions that occur no longer take place between city and country. The principal contradiction is shifted to the urban phenomenon itself: between the centrality of power and other forms of centrality, between the "wealth-power" center and the periphery, between integration and segregation.

A complete examination of the critical phase would far exceed the scope of this book. As an example, what remains of the classic notions of history and historicity? The critical phase can leave neither these concepts nor the corresponding reality intact. Does the extension of the urban phenomenon, the formation of a time-space differential on a global scale, have any relationship to what is still called "historicity"?

This phase is accompanied by the emergence of complex entities, new functions and structures, but this does not mean that the old ones necessarily disappear. For this reason, what is called for is a repeated, and repeatedly refined, analysis of the relations between form and content. Here I've limited myself to the barest outline, consisting of a handful of markers and directional arrows. What is most important is to demonstrate that the dialectic method can exercise its revenge. And why not? Swept aside by the strategy (ideological and institutional) of the industrial period and corporate rationalism, replaced by an advocacy of the operational, deprecated by procedures that are reductive and generalizing (primarily structuralism), dialectical thought reasserts its rights. As I stated earlier, the key issue, in the fullest and most accurate sense of the word, that of centrality, demands a dialectic analysis. The study of the logic of space leads to the study of its contradictions (and those of space-time). Without that analysis, the solutions to the problem are merely dissimulated strategies, hidden beneath an apparent scientificity. On the theoretical level, one of the severest critiques of urbanism as a body of doctrine (not altogether successful) is that it harbors a socio-logic and a strategy, while it evacuates dialectical thought in general and the dialectical movements specific to urbanism in particular—in other words, internal contradictions, both old and new (one aggravating and masking the other).

Is the urban phenomenon the *total social phenomenon* long sought for by sociologists? Yes and no. Yes, in the sense that it tends toward totality without ever achieving it, that it is essentially totalizing (centrality) but that this totality is never effected. Yes, in the sense that no partial determinism, no fragmentary knowledge can exhaust it; it is simultaneously historical, demographic, geographic, economic, sociologic, psychologic, semiologic, and so on. It "is" that and more (thing or non-thing) besides: *form,* for example. In other words, a void, but one that demands or calls forth a content. If the urban is total, it is not total in the way a thing can be, as content that has been amassed, but in the way that thought is, which continues its activity of concentration endlessly but can never hold or maintain that state of concentration, which assembles elements continuously and discovers what it has assembled through a new and different form of concentration. Centrality defines the u-topic (that which has no place and searches for it). The u-topic defines centrality.

But neither the separation of fragment and content nor their confused union can define (and therefore express) the urban phenomenon. For it incorporates a *total reading*, combining the vocabularies (partial readings) of geographers, demographers, economists, sociologists, semiologists, and others. These readings take place on different levels. The phenomenon cannot be defined by their sum or synthesis or superposition. In this sense, it is not a totality. Similarly, it overcomes the separation between accident and necessity, but their synthesis doesn't determine it, assuming such synthesis can be determined. This is simply a repetition of the paradox of the urban phenomenon, a paradox that in no way gives it precedence over the fundamental paradox of thought and awareness. For it is undoubtedly the same. The urban is specific: it is localized and focused. It is locally intensified and doesn't exist without that localization, or center. Thought and thinking don't take place unless they are themselves localized. The specificity of the fact, the event, is a given. And, consequently, a requirement. Near order occurs around a point, taken as a (momentary) center, which is produced by practice and can be grasped through analysis. This defines an isotopy. At the same time, the urban phenomenon is colossal; its prodigious extension-expansion cannot be constrained. While encompassing near order, a *distant order* groups distinct specificities, assembles them according to their differences (heterotopies). But isotopy and heterotopy clash everywhere and always, engendering an *elsewhere*. Although initially indispensable, the *transformed* centrality that results will be reabsorbed into the fabric of space-time. In this way the dialectical movement of the specific and the colossal, of place and non-place (elsewhere), of urban order and urban disorder assumes form (reveals itself as form).

The urban is not produced like agriculture or industry. Yet, as an act that assembles and distributes, it does create. Similarly, manufacturing at one time became a productive force and economic category simply because it brought together labor and tools (technology), which were formerly dispersed. In this sense, the urban phenomenon contains a praxis (urban practice). Its form, as such, cannot be reduced to other forms (it is not isomorphous with other forms and structures), but it absorbs and transforms them.

The procedure for accessing urban reality as a form is reversed once the process is complete. In this way we can use linguistics to define isotopy and heterotopy. Once they have been identified in the urban text, these concepts assume a different meaning. Isn't it because human habitations assume the form that they do that they can be recognized in discourse? The urban is associated with a discourse and a route, or pathway. And it is for this reason, or formal cause, that there are different discourses and pathways in language. One cannot be separated from the other. Although different, language and dwelling are indissolubly combined. Is it surprising then that there is a *paradigm* of the urban (high and low, private and public), just as there is for habiting (open and closed, intimate and public), although neither the urban nor habiting can be defined by a simple discourse or by a system? If there is any logic inherent in the urban and the habiting it implies, it is not the logic of a system (or a subject or an object). It is the logic of thought (subject) that looks for a content (object). It is for this reason that our understanding of the urban requires that we simultaneously abandon our illusions of subjectivity (representation, ideology) and objectivity (causality, partial determinism).

Although the urban consolidates differences and engenders difference within the things it brings together, it cannot be defined as a system of differences. Either the word "system" implies fulfillment and closure, intelligibility through completion, or it implies nothing more than a certain kind of coherence. But the urban phenomenon is made manifest as movement. Therefore, it cannot achieve closure. The centrality and the dialectical contradiction it implies exclude closure, that is to say, immobility. Even if language appears to be a closed system, the use of language and the production of discourse shatter this perception. Consequently, we cannot define the urban by means of a system (definite); for example, as a series of deviations around invariant points. In fact, the very concept precludes our ability to mandate anything that reduces or suppresses differences. Rather, it would imply the freedom to produce differences (to differ and invent that which differs).

The urban consolidates. As a form, the urban transforms what it brings together (concentrates). It consciously creates difference where no awareness of difference existed: what was only distinct, what was once attached to particularities in the field. It consolidates everything, including determinisms, heterogeneous materials and contents, prior order and disorder, conflict, preexisting communications and forms of communication. As a transforming form, the urban destructures and restructures its elements: the messages and codes that arise in the industrial and agrarian domains.

The urban also contains a negative power, which can easily appear harmful. Nature, a desire, and what we call culture (and what the industrial era dissociated from nature, while during predominately agrarian periods, nature and culture were indissoluble) are reworked and combined in urban society. Heterogeneous, if not heteroclite, these contents are put to the test. Thus, by way of analogy, agricultural exploitation (the farm) and the enterprise (which came into existence with the rise of manufacturing) are put to the test, are transformed, and are incorporated in new forms within the urban fabric. We could consider this a form of second-order creativity *(poiesis)*, agricultural and industrial production being forms of first-order creativity. This does not mean that the urban phenomenon can be equated with second-order discourse, metalanguage, exegesis, or commentary on industrial production. No, second-order creation and the secondary naturality of the urban serve to *multiply* rather than reduce or reflect creative activity. This raises the issue of an activity that produces (creates) meanings from elements that already possess signification (rather than units similar to phonemes, sounds or signs devoid of signification). From this point of view, the urban would create situations and acts just as it does objects.

There is no model for determining the urban through its elements or conditions (what it brings together—contents and activities). Models borrowed from the fields of energy (devices that capture finite, but considerable, quantities of energy) and information (which uses minute amounts of energy) are also inappropriate here. In other words, if we want to find a model, an analytic study of the urban can supply them. But in practice, this has more to do with a path (sense and direction, orientation and horizon) than a model.

This means that there is nothing harmonious about the urban as form and reality, for it also incorporates conflict, including class conflict. What is more, it can only be conceptualized in opposition to segregation, which attempts to resolve conflicts by separating the elements in space. This segregation produces a disaggregation of material and social life. To avoid contradiction, to achieve a purported sense of harmony, a certain form of urbanism prefers the disaggregation of the social bond. The urban presents itself as a place of conflict and confrontation, a unity of contradictions. It is in this sense that the concept incorporates dialectical thought (deeply modified, it is true, because it is now attached to a mental and social form rather than a historical content).

We could therefore define the urban as a place where conflicts are *expressed*, reversing the separation of places where expression disappears, where silence reigns, where the signs of separation are established. The urban could also be defined as a place of *desire*, where desire emerges from need, where it is concentrated because it is recognized, where Eros and Logos can (possibly) be found side by side. Nature (desire) and culture (categorized needs and induced facticity) come together during the course of a mutual self-criticism that engenders impassioned dialogues. In this way the immature and premature character of the human being is formed, handed over to the struggles of Eros and Logos, although this formation is not necessary for the development of the mature adult. The urban as a practical medium would, paradoxically, serve a pedagogical role that is quite different from the customary pedagogy based on the authority of acquired knowledge, the finished adult.

From this point of view, the industrial era (in other words, what passes for industrial society) looks quite different than it looked to itself. From its own perspective, it was productive and creative, in control of nature, substituting the freedom of production for the determinism of matter. In fact—in truth—it was radically contradictory and conflictual. Rather than dominating nature, industry ravaged it, destroyed it completely. Claiming to substitute a consistent rationality for the chaos of spontaneity, it separated and dissociated everything it touched, it destroyed connections by instituting a reign of homogeneous order. For industry, the means became an end and the end a means: production became strategy, productivism a philosophy, the state a divinity. The order and the disorder of the industrial era reproduced the earlier, blood-filled chaos; indeed they aggravated it. Ideologues (especially urban ideologues) think they can still base the principle of superior organization on the industrial era and its rationality. For them the problem is to overcome that order and disorder and create a higher order, but from established principles. Extending the principles of the enterprise unchanged to society as a whole is a strategy that has now been judged and condemned. Because there is something else (a different non-thing) that we must acknowledge, that calls everything into question, that is itself question . . .

The separation brought about by industrial rationality also occurs among a number of subsystems: values, decisions, models of action and behavior. Could the pluralism of those subsystems accommodate or create a certain coherence? The sense of cohesion of the whole appeared to come from the ideology of the enterprise and the ideology of the state. And yet, something else was needed so that this juxtaposition of isolated functions—deciding, wishing, projecting—could operate. Sociologists were right when they isolated those subsystems as being functionally and structurally distinct. They failed because they failed to show how that order and its immanent disorder, those units and their disjunctions, could contain a self-regulatory mechanism and constitute a whole, and in some cases a totality. It would be easy to show where the reductive approach of American and Soviet (to the extent that we are familiar with them) ideologues failed. However, this immanent cohesion could only arise from a logic. This socio-logic was hidden behind or beneath sociology. It was and still is the logic of commodity and the world of commodities, dissimulated (absent) *as such* in the language of commodities yet still present in every object that is bought, sold, and consumed. It was also, and still is, the implacable logic of the state, of power conceived (or conceiving itself) as omniscient and omnipresent—logic that was also dissimulated as such, beneath the ethical prestige of the state.

The logic of repressive space reestablished coherence. This resulted in the complication and anxiety inherent in a society that was destroyed, slowly but surely, by urban society and its transparent logic, a logic that comes into view as soon as we are able to express it. Similarly, we need only formulate those other socio-logics for them to disappear (this is theoretically self-evident).

We can now identify and formulate a number of *urban laws*. These are not positive laws, the laws associated with an "order of orders," or a model of equilibrium or growth that should be followed or imitated, the laws of an initial affirmation from which consequences can be deduced, or some final analysis that would result in various propositions. No, these are primarily, essentially, negative laws and precepts.

1. We must break down the barriers that block the path and maintain the urban field in thrall to the blinding-blinded (especially in terms of the quantitative aspects of growth).

2. We must put an end to separation, to the separation between people and things, which brings about multiform segregations, the separation between messages, information, codes, and subcodes (in short, the forms of separation that block qualitative development). But in the existing order, what separates imagines itself to be solid; what dissociates is conscious of its power; what divides judges itself to be positive.

3. We must overcome the obstacles that enhance the opacity of relationships and the contrasts between transparency and opacity, that relegate differences to distinct (separate) particularities, that restrict them to a prefabricated space, that mask the polyvalence of ways of living in urban society (modalities and modulations of the everyday and habiting), that outlaw the transgression of norms that stipulate separations.

These negative laws in turn imply a number of positive laws.

positive laws:

1. The urban (urban life, the life of urban society) already implies the substitution of custom for contract. Contract law determines the frameworks of exchange and of reciprocity in exchange. This law comes into being in agrarian societies once they begin to exchange their relative surpluses and (once the world of commodities is in place) achieves its highest expression in logic and language. However, use, in the urban, comprises custom and privileges custom over contract. The use of urban objects (this sidewalk, this street, this crosswalk, this light fixture) is customary, not contractual, unless we wish to postulate the existence of a permanent quasi contract or pseudo-contract for sharing those objects and reducing violence to a minimum. This does not, however, imply that the contract system cannot be improved or transformed.

2. The conception of the urban also strives for the *re-appropriation* by human beings of their conditions in time, in space, and in objects—conditions that were, and continue to be, taken away from them so that their recovery will be deferred until after buying and selling have taken place.

   (Is it reasonable to assume that time—the place of values—and space—the medium of exchange—can be reunited in a higher unity, the urban? Yes, providing we clearly point out what everyone already knows: that this unity is a u-topia, a non-place, a possible-impossible, but one that gives meaning to the possible, to action. The space of exchange and the time of values, the space of goods and the supreme good, namely time, cannot be articulated and go their own way, reflecting the incoherence of so-called industrial society. Creating space-time unity would be a possible definition, one among many, of the urban and urban society.)

3. Politically, this perspective cannot be conceived without extensive self-management of production and the enterprise within territorial units. A difficult proposition. The term "politically" is a source of confusion because generalized self-management implies the withering away of the state and the end of politics as such. In this sense, the incompatibility between the state and the urban is radical in nature. The state can only prevent the urban from taking shape. The state has to control the urban phenomenon, not to bring it to fruition but to retard its development, to push it in the direction of institutions that extend to society as a whole, through exchange and the market, the types of organization and management found in the enterprise, institutions developed during periods of growth, where the emphasis is given to quantitative (quantifiable) objectives. But the urban can only establish and serve "habiting" by reversing the state order and the strategy that organizes space globally, through constraint and homogenization, thereby absorbing the subordinate levels of the urban and habiting.

As I have tried to show, urbanism is a mask and a tool: a mask for the state and political action, a tool of interests that are dissimulated within a strategy and a socio-logic. Urbanism does not try to model space as a work of art. It does not even try to do so in keeping with its technological imperatives, as it claims. The space it creates is political.

Conclusion

Throughout this book I have examined various aspects of the urban problematic. However, one of the most disturbing problems still remains: the extraordinary passivity of the people most directly involved, those who are affected by projects, influenced by strategies. Why this silence on the part of "users"? Why the uncertain mutterings about "aspirations"—assuming anyone even bothers to consider them? What exactly is behind this strange situation?

In this book I have criticized urbanism as ideology and institution, representation and will, pressure and repression, because it establishes a repressive space that is represented as objective, scientific, and neutral. It is obvious that this explanation, although necessary, is incomplete. It is only one part of the explanation or interpretation of one paradoxical fact among a number of paradoxes. To conclude, I would like to tie up some loose ends in my argument and add a few additional thoughts on urbanism.

1. Couldn't the passivity of those who inhabit, who could and should "dwell poetically" (Hölderlin), be compared to the strange impasse that architectural and urbanist thought

181

has come up against? It is as if their projects were under the influence of some strange curse. It seems that the only progress they have made involves the use of graphics and technology. The imagination is hampered in its flight. The authors of these projects have clearly not succeeded in locating the intersection of the following two principles: *(a)* there is no thought without u-topia, without an exploration of the possible, of the elsewhere; *(b)* there is no thought without reference to practice (here the practice of habiting and use, but what if the inhabitant and the user remain silent?).

The massive involvement of those affected would alter this state of affairs. Would it enable those thoughts and projects to cross the threshold before which they seem to hesitate? Possibly. But that involvement has never taken place. Here and there we see scattered signs of renewed interest. But there has been no trace of any political movement—that is, the politicization of the problems and objectives of "construction."

Where does this blockage come from? The question cuts to the heart of the matter. The mechanism is fairly obvious on the theoretical plane: concrete space has been replaced with abstract space. Concrete space is the space of habiting: gestures and paths, bodies and memory, symbols and meanings, the difficult maturation of the immature-premature (of the "human being"), contradictions and conflicts between desires and needs, and so forth. This concrete content, time inscribed in space, an unconscious poiesis that misunderstands its own conditions, is also misunderstood by thought. Instead, it takes off into the abstract space of vision, of geometry. The architect who draws and the urbanist who composes a block plan look down on their "objects," buildings and neighborhoods, from above and afar. These designers and draftsmen move within a space of paper and ink. Only after this nearly complete *reduction* of the everyday do they return to the scale of lived experience. They are convinced they have captured it even though they carry out their plans and projects within a second-order abstraction. They've shifted from lived experience to the abstract, projecting this abstraction back onto lived experience. This twofold substitution and negation creates an illusory sense of affirmation: the return to "real" life. In this way the blinding-blinded operates on a field that may appear to be illuminated but is in fact blind.

How can we put an end to this ideo-logic of substitution, hidden beneath technical arguments, justified by professional skills, without the rebellion of lived experience, of the everyday, of praxis? The technicians and specialists who "act" are unaware that their so-called objective space is in fact ideo-logic and repressive.

2. There are historical reasons for this situation. The town, the city, has fascinated people for centuries. They have developed a sense of parish pump politics, or parochialism. Only in this sense did they take an interest in the organization of space, form groups that produced space. Generally, these were "notables," who, quite naturally, took an interest in the morphological and social framework of their "interests." This attitude has far from disappeared in towns and small cities. However, it has lost or is losing its most powerful incentives. Its offensive, productive attitude (of social space and time, that is to say, the use of time) has changed into a defensive attitude, has become passive. Battles are fought against the encroachments of a central authority and state pressure. But we know that the real problems lie elsewhere, that the most important decisions are made elsewhere. This creates a sense of disappointment in urban reality because we know that there is something outdated about the reality of the town or small city, that it is becoming an embarrassment. How can we make the transition from the city, which maintains its image, which has a heart, a face, a "soul," to *urban society*, without a long period of disorientation?

Between 1920 and 1930, Russia experienced a tremendous

spurt of creative activity. Quite amazingly, Russian society, turned upside down through revolution, managed to produce superstructures (out of the depths) of astonishing novelty. This occurred in just about every field of endeavor, including politics, architecture, and urbanism. These superstructures were far in advance of the existing structures (social relations) and base (productive forces). The existing base and superstructures would have had to follow, make up for their delay, and reach the level of the superstructures that had come into existence through the process of revolutionary creativity. This was a key problem for Lenin during his last years. Today, however, it has become painfully obvious that those structures and the "base" did a poor job of catching up. The superstructures produced by revolutionary genius collapsed on top of a base (peasant, backward) that had been badly or inadequately modified. Isn't this the great drama of our era? Architectural and urbanist thought cannot arise from thought or theory alone (urbanistic, sociological, economic). It came into being during this total phenomenon known as revolution. The creations of the revolutionary period in the Soviet Union quickly disappeared; they were destroyed and then forgotten. So why did it take forty years, why did we have to wait until today (an age that some claim is characterized by speed, acceleration, vertigo) and the work of Anatole Kopp to acknowledge the achievements of architectural and urban thought and practice in the Soviet Union?[1] In spite of the favorable circumstances (in France, in 1968, there also occurred a "total phenomenon" that was, to some extent, comparable to the phenomena that took place in Russia between 1920 and 1930), it is not clear that this knowledge has been assimilated. We live with the consequences: the remains of revolutions buried under the remains of technology.

There are several historical reasons for passivity and obstruction. And aren't we, faced with the urban phenomenon, in a situation comparable to the one faced a century ago by those who had to accommodate the growth of industrial phenomena? Those who hadn't read Marx—which is to say, nearly everyone—saw only chaos, unrelated facts. This was true not only of "ordinary" people, but "cultivated" individuals as well, including economists. All they saw were separate units, enterprises, each of which was under the control of a manager (boss, owner, entrepreneur). Before their eyes, society was being atomized, dissociating into individuals and fragments. Even the market seemed like a series or collection of unconnected accidents. Since totality was not a part of thought or action, since the concept of planning was still somewhat vague, there were no objections to this atomistic and molecular vision of the social. There was no way to account for the facts, to act on them. Isn't the same true today with respect to the urban phenomenon and urban society? We don't know how to approach them. Contemporary thought and action can only accommodate empty spaces and the void of space. Plenitude is resistant. It escapes our grasp. Or rather, it fragments indefinitely before any thought or action that attempts to comprehend it. Thought floats between a self-annihilating plenitude and the void that defies it.

The political reasons for passivity need to be taken seriously. Enormous pressure is at work to maintain awareness within fixed boundaries. Ideologically, technically, and politically, the quantitative has become rule, norm, and value. How can we escape the quantifiable? Even in business, bodies that represent the working class express their demands and aspirations in quantifiable terms: salary and work week. The qualitative is worn down. Anything that cannot be quantified is eliminated. The generalized terrorism of the quantifiable accentuates the efficiency of repressive space, amplifies it without fear and without reproach, all the more so because of its self-justifying nature (ideo-logic), its apparent scientificity. In this situation, since the quantitative is never seriously questioned, the working class has no scope for political action. In terms of urbanism, it can offer nothing of consequence.

In spite of its inability to construct a body of doctrine, in spite of its internal discord (between humanists and technocrats, private entrepreneurs and government representatives), urbanism reflects this overall situation and plays an active role in applying ideo-logic and political pressure. This much is obvious. But it can only be avoided through an ongoing process of self-criticism.

3. What about the theoretical aspects of passivity? These are associated with the fragmentation of the urban phenomenon. As I indicated earlier, there is a paradox here: the urban phenomenon can only be comprehended as a totality, but its totality cannot be grasped. It escapes us. It is always elsewhere. Little by little, I've tried to elaborate the nature of this paradox, which signifies centrality and the dialectic of centrality, urban praxis, and finally urban revolution. This threefold character, rejected by ideology and positivist pseudoscientificity, justifies the most extreme fragmentation, motivates the most cynical forms of compartmentalization. Some pseudoconcepts, which appear to be precise (operational) and global, legitimate fragmentation and compartmentalization. Take the pseudoconcept of the *environment,* for example. What exactly does it refer to? Nature? A milieu? This much is obvious but trivial. The surroundings? Yes, but which? No one seems to know. The city has an environment; it's called the countryside. Individuals have an environment: it's the succession of envelopes, skins, and shells (Abraham Moles) that contain them, from their habits to their neighborhood.[2] The apartment block and the neighborhood have their environments and serve as environments in turn. Is it the city's boundary or the city as boundary that we refer to as an environment? If not, why not? As soon as we try to be specific, we turn to a specialist, a technician. Thus, there is a geographic environment, a site, landscape, ecosystem. There

is a historical environment, an economic and sociologic environment. The semiologist describes symbolic systems and the signs that environ individuals and groups. The psychosociologist describes the groups that serve as environments for individuals. And so on. In the end, we have access to a number of partial descriptions and analytic statements. We spread them out on the table before us or dump them all into the same sack. That's our environment. In fact, the image is borrowed from ecological and morphological, which is to say limited, description, and this has been extended carelessly because it is simple and pliable. It has been used for the conventional and well-known (although officially unknown as such) operations of extrapolation and reduction.

The concept of infrastructure, although more technical, yields the same result: isolated functions, projected separately onto the terrain; analytic fragments of a global reality that the very process destroys. Urban life is said to be located within diverse and diversified infrastructures that satisfy any number of problems. In fact, functional location overlooks so large a number of elements and so rarely achieves its goals that it is hardly worth the trouble to criticize it from the point of view of theory. Similarly, we need only mention the growing number of authorities, skills, services, and offices associated with the separate "elements" of urban reality. Here, too, the only limits the bureaucrat and bureaucratic fragmentation encounter are internal. These continue to proliferate until they stop functioning, caught up in the inextricable interlocking of skills that are themselves localized in offices. This situation would be comic if it didn't imply a practice: the segregation, projected onto the terrain, of *all* the isolated elements of the *whole*.

4. There are sociological reasons, as well, for this phenomenon, namely the passivity (the lack of participation) of those affected, which the ideology of participation will in no way change. We have a long history of delegating our

interests to our representatives. Political representatives have not always played their part, and sometimes their part has been eliminated. So to whom should we delegate power and the representation of practical and social life? To experts and those with skills. They in turn can confer with one another and rule on everything that concerns a functionalized "habitat." Habiting and the inhabitant play no role in their decisions. Decisions are placed in the hands of decision makers. Activity withdraws to the everyday, to static space, to the reification that is initially endured, then accepted.

How could the user not feel excluded from the dialogue (assuming there is dialogue) between the architect and the urbanist? Sometimes these are found in the same individual, sometimes they are separate, and sometimes they disagree. Frequently, they establish a contract, a quasi contract, or a gentleman's agreement between them. What is the best situation for the user? A not-too-violent conflict between these two individuals. How often is the user present to take advantage of this circumstance? Rarely.

Who is this user? It's as if they (the skilled, the agents, the authorities) had so excluded *use* for the sake of *exchange* that this use came to be confused with usury. So how is the user perceived? As a fairly repulsive character who soils whatever is sold to him new and fresh, who breaks, who causes wear, who fortunately fulfills the function of making the replacement of a thing inevitable, who successfully carries out the process of obsolescence. Which is hardly an excuse.

Notes

The French text of *The Urban Revolution* was published in 1970. The original notes are reproduced here but may refer to more recent editions of cited references.

1. From the City to Urban Society

1. The bibliography on the subject is now rather extensive. The initial research was sparked by a well-known article entitled "Asiaticus," published in *Rinascita* (Rome), 1963. The standard reference still remains K. A. Wittfogel, *Oriental Despotism: A Comparative Study of Total Power* (New Haven, Conn.: Yale University Press, 1957). See also the articles by J. Chesneaux in *La Pensée,* nos. 114 and 122, and M. Godelier in *Les Temps modernes,* May 1965, and Marx's *Grundrisse* and *Capital.*

2. ["Habiting" is my translation of the highly unusual form *l'habiter.* Although the term is far from euphonious, even somewhat jarring, it accords well with the author's usage. Lefebvre employs an infinitive *(habiter)* that has been made to serve as a noun *(l'habiter).* Such forms obviously contravene correct grammatical use—even in French. Although Lefebvre doesn't explicitly say so, the term is derived from Heidegger's use of the verb *wohnen,* from which *das Wohnen,* the verbal noun, is formed. This in turn has been translated as "dwelling"

(the gerundive form rather than the noun synonymous with "house" or "abode"). One of the underlying reasons for my decision to translate *l'habiter* as "habiting" is the author's frequent juxtaposition of *l'habiter* with French *habitat,* which is paralleled in English "habiting" and "habitat." Moreover, both "to habit" (the verb from which "habiting" is formed) and French *habiter* are derived from the same Latin infinitive, *habitare.* An additional argument for the use of "habiting" is its unexpectedness (a verbal noun used as an ordinary noun) for the reader.

Additional support for this translation can be found in Heidegger himself, at least as he has been interpreted by his translators. In "Building, Dwelling, Thinking," Heidegger writes, "Building as dwelling, that is, as being on the earth, however, remains for man's everyday experience that which is from the outset *'habitual'*—we *inhabit* it" (my emphasis). "Habiting" captures some of the echoes of the terms "habitual" and "inhabiting," which stem from similar roots: "habitual" from Latin *habitus,* "inhabit" from Latin *inhabitare (in + habitare).*

One criticism that has been leveled at the use of "dwell" as a translation of *wohnen* is that the term implies a sense of temporal duration, something Heidegger did not intend. "Habiting" is less durative and therefore more consonant with Heidegger's own usage. For examples of the use of "dwelling" in Heidegger, see *Being and Time,* trans. Joan Stambaugh (Albany, N.Y.: State University of New York Press, 1996), and "Building, Dwelling, Thinking," in *Poetry, Language, Thought,* trans. Albert Hofstadter (New York: Harper Colophon Books, 1971).—*Trans.*]

2. Blind Field

1. Cf. J. T. Desanti, *Idéalités mathématiques* (Paris: Seuil, 1968).

2. *Isotopy* is defined as "a redundant set of semantic categories that makes it possible to read a story as something uniform, this reading being the result of partial readings of the utterances after resolution of their ambiguities, this resolution itself being guided by the search for a single reading" (Algirdas Julien Greimas, "Eléments pour une théorie de l'interprétation du récit," in *Communication,* no. 8, 30; see also *Structural Semantics,* 96). The concept is thus associated with a reading of urban space (and the time inscribed in this space). This space, which is more or less legible in the image and on maps of the

city, can be read in various ways. It gives rise to different vocabularies and different types of discourse, just as it encourages recourse to different paths through the city. The term "isotopy" and its correlate "heterotopy" indicate the suitability of bringing together a plurality of discourses and vocabularies by situating them in one place. These paths through the city can engender numerous discourses with varying forms, functions, and urban structures. Who is talking? Who is acting? Who is moving in space? A subject (individual or collective) who participates in social relations (ownership, production, consumption). The description of isotopies and heterotopies goes hand in hand with the analysis of the acts and situations of these subjects and their relation to objects populating the urban space. This leads to the discovery, or rather re-cognition, of the presence-absence that contributes to the population of urban space, of an elsewhere, a utopia (a place without place that has not taken place).

3. Using borrowed concepts and terms, we can say that the urban (as opposed to urbanism, whose ambiguity is gradually revealed) rises above the horizon, slowly occupies an epistemological field, and becomes the episteme of an epoch. History and the historic grow further apart. Psychoanalysis and linguistics, like economy and politics, reach their apogee and begin to decline. The urban begins its ascendance. The important thing is not to classify the fields, the domains, the topoi of the understanding but to influence their movement. We can, if we prefer, refer to this activity as "theoretical practice," but it has nothing in common with a scientism that asserts itself as a criterion, pushing aside the "lived" and praxis.

3. The Urban Phenomenon

1. The urban center displays the following characteristics: the simultaneous presence of elements in the urban inventory (objects, people) that are fixed and separate within the periphery based on a (redundant) order, the interaction of these elements and, consequently, disorder and maximum information. This creates complexification with respect to the periphery as well as the risks and dangers arising from this influx. Decentrality is fixed in redundancy. The analytic and formal (mathematical) study of these phenomena runs the risk of masking the *dialectic of centrality.* No single center is self-sufficient or

sufficient. Saturation makes this impossible. It directs us toward a *different* center, a *different* centrality.

2. See the work of Christopher Alexander in *Architecture, Mouvement, Continuité* (1967), no. 1.

3. This is the biggest stumbling block for the application of post-Saussurian linguistics and the Saussurian model to the theory of myths and mythology, literature, stories, and so forth. See in particular the work of Lévi-Strauss and Roland Barthes. This is why other models are needed. [N. Trubetzkoy (1890–1938) was one of the founders of the Prague School of structuralism.—*Trans.*]

4. See R. Boudon: *The Uses of Structuralism,* trans. Michalina Vaughan (London: Heinemann, 1971).

5. [Louis Bolk (1866–1930) was a Dutch anatomist who formulated a theory of "fetalization," according to which humans developed by retaining the juvenile features of their ancestors. Unlike those of primates, human features are assumed to be fetal conditions that have become permanent.—*Trans.*]

4. Levels and Dimensions

1. Friedrich Nietzsche, *Thus Spake Zarathustra,* part 3, "On Virtue that Makes Small," trans. Walter Kaufmann (Harmondsworth, England: Penguin Books, 1978).

2. This grid has been constructed and verified based on information collected in Kyoto, Japan, a remarkable urban space, where city architects and urbanists supplied the author with the needed information: historic, cadastral, demographic, et cetera. During my all-too-brief stay in Japan (approximately two months), I attempted a first approximation for a study of urban and architectural space in the country, using the analytic categories of Western thought. The potential advantages of such a study, which would have included a knowledge of ideograms and their associated time-space components, as well as Asian modes of production and their variants (including an understanding of China), were barely touched upon. This is a historic space, which predates capitalism and industry, but is highly complex.

An analysis of space (or rather of time-space) undertaken here would focus on:

a. the principle of interaction, interpenetration, and superposition of spaces (paths)
b. the concepts of polyfunctionality and transfunctionality
c. the dialectics of centrality
d. the contradictions of space
e. the concept of the production of the space of (time-space), and so on

In light of this sequence (proceeding from the abstract to the concrete, from logistics to the dialectic exploration of the contradictions of space), can we really talk about an urbanistic epistemology? Possibly, but only with certain reservations. Developing the supposedly definitive "cores" or "centers" of formal knowledge is never without risk. Rational solidity and "purity" tend toward a strange kind of segregation, even in terms of theory.

3. See Anatole Kopp, *Town and Revolution: Soviet Architecture and City Planning, 1917–1935,* trans. Thomas E. Burton (New York: Braziller, 1970).

4. [Yona Friedman was born in Budapest, Hungary, in 1923 and graduated from the Technological Institute of Haifa, Israel. He has lived and worked in Paris since 1956. In 1958, he published his manifesto, *L'Architecture mobile.* He is the author of a number of urban projects promoting the idea of a spatial architecture that implicates the participation of the users.—*Trans.*]

5. See the texts from the 1919 Manifesto and the *Bauhaus* review (no. 4, 1928), which appeared in the Bauhaus exhibition at the Museum of Modern Art in Paris, 1969, as well as the catalog for the exhibition.

6. My remarks are aimed at Roger Garaudy and his brand of "Marxist humanism," as well as at Louis Althusser (*For Marx,* translated from the French by Ben Brewster [New York: Pantheon Books, 1969]) and Lucien Sève (*Marxism and the Theory of Human Personality* [London: Lawrence and Wishart, 1975]) and others. It is especially strange to follow in Marxist (so-called Marxist) thought the consequences of this philosophizing attitude, the efforts to maintain and sustain it, to retain its abstraction as the private property of an apparatus (which also ensures the privatization of ideas).

By studying social relationships without considering places (which are filled with these relationships) and morphology (material), aren't we at risk of applying a purely *idealist* approach? The attitude of these philosophers, who claim to be materialists, can only be explained by the ideological power of the apparatus.

5. Urban Myths and Ideologies

1. I don't want to belabor a point already highlighted but left unresolved: how do already signifying units become part of other units? Is meaning transformed, invented, or created? Are heretofore unknown combinations now brought to light through new relationships? Or is it only metalanguage, a discourse about an initial discourse? I feel that the first solution, effected through the relationship between text and context, is the most reasonable.

2 . [Anatole Kopp is the author of *Town and Revolution: Soviet Architecture and City Planning, 1917–1935,* trans. Thomas E. Burton (New York: Braziller [1970]), and *Constructivist Architecture in the USSR,* trans. Sheila de Vallée (London: Academy Editions; New York: St. Martin's Press, 1985).—*Trans.*]

6. Urban Form

1. This theory of form envelops and develops the analysis I provided in *Right to the City,* ed. Joan Ockman (New York: Columbia Books of Architecture/Rizzoli International Publications, 1993). In *Right to the City,* the city is understood as *(a)* a (spatial) object, *(b)* mediation (between near and distant order), *(c)* a work (similar to the work of art, formed by a group). Form unifies these three aspects of the city. The "right to the city" becomes the right to centrality, the right to not be excluded from urban form, if only with respect to the decisions and actions of power. I also demonstrated

a. that the tree, that is, a graph of the tree, is a rigorous, limiting structure that only provides access to predetermined pathways
b. that this structure is both mental and social
c. that it projects onto the terrain a bureaucratic conception (hierarchic) of society
d. that its "scientificity" dissimulates an ideology
e. that this schema is reductive of urban reality
f. that it is generally adopted by urbanists as representative of the urban order, although it is segregating

These topics will be discussed in further detail in my *Théorie de l'espace urbain.*

7. Toward an Urban Strategy

1. [Georges Gurvitch (1894–1965) was a French sociologist born in Novorossiysk, Russia. He is the author of numerous works of sociology, including *The Social Frameworks of Knowledge,* trans. Margaret A. Thompson and Kenneth A. Thompson (New York: Harper and Row [1971]), and *Sociology of Law* (London: Paul, Trench, Trubner, 1947).—*Trans.*]

2. [The Marais, one of the many historic districts of Paris, is located in the third and fourth arrondissements. The area became one of the most fashionable parts of Paris in the seventeenth century following the construction of the Place des Vosges and was soon populated by the nobility and wealthy Parisians. The region became a center of art and culture. However, the Marais experienced a period of decline that lasted from the eighteenth to the mid–twentieth century, sparked by the relocation of many of its residents to the more fashionable Faubourg Saint-Honoré and Faubourg Saint-Germain. These new neighborhoods offered light and open space, which were in short supply in the Marais's narrow streets and small courtyards. After the flight of the aristocracy, the area was occupied primarily by light industry and artisans, and it housed a large Jewish community, primarily along Rue des Rosiers. The Marais was classified a historic district in 1962, when efforts at restoration were begun. In recent years it has—once again—become one of the most fashionable neighborhoods of central Paris.—*Trans.*]

8. The Urban Illusion

1. [Bruno Bauer (1809–82) was a German rationalist philosopher and theologian. Prior to the 1848 revolution, he was a Left Hegelian and developed a republican interpretation of Hegel's ideas. As a theologian, he described religion as a form of alienation. After the revolution, Bauer repudiated Hegel and predicted a crisis of European civilization. His writings are said to have influenced Nietzsche, Engels, and Karl Kautsky. Bauer was a prolific writer, but little of his work has been translated into English. The following, however, are available: *Christ*

and the Caesars: The Origin of Christianity from Romanized Greek Culture, trans. Frank E. Schacht (Charleston, S.C.: Davidonis, c. 1998), and *The Trumpet of the Last Judgement against Hegel the Atheist and Antichrist: An Ultimatum,* trans. Lawrence Stepelevich (Lewiston, N.Y.: Mellen Press, 1989).

Max Stirner (1806–56) is a pseudonym for Johann Kaspar Schmidt, a German anti-statist philosopher in whose writings many anarchists of the late nineteenth and the twentieth centuries found ideological inspiration. He is sometimes regarded as a source of twentieth-century existentialism. Like Bauer, Stirner started out as a Left Hegelian but attacked what he perceived as the radicalism of Bauer, Feuerbach, and Marx. He thought the only reality was that of the individual ego. His best-known work in English is *The Ego and His Own: The Case of the Individual against Authority,* trans. Steven T. Byington, ed. James J. Martin (New York: Dover [1973]).—*Trans.*]

2. [W. W. Rostow, American economic historian, developed a five-stage economic growth model that incorporated what he termed "takeoff," which was based on Western (primarily British) economic development in the eighteenth and nineteenth centuries. See *The Stages of Economic Growth: A Non-Communist Manifesto* (New York: Cambridge University Press, 1962).—*Trans.*]

Conclusion

1. [For Kopp, see ch. 5, n. 1.—*Trans.*]

2. [Abraham A. Moles (1920–92) was an influential French engineer and sociologist who was head of research at the CNRS (Centre National de la Recherche Scientifique) (1945–54) and later directed Hermann Scherchen's Laboratory of Electronic Music in Switzerland. He taught in several countries and founded the Institute of Social Psychology in Strasbourg in 1966. He is the author of numerous publications, including *Information Theory and Esthetic Perception,* trans. Joel F. Cohen (Urbana: University of Illinois Press, 1966).—*Trans.*]

Henri Lefebvre (1901–1991) was a noted French philosopher and sociologist. His treatment of modern urban society resulted in the production of several works that have become classics of urban studies, and he was among the first scholars to recognize the implications of alienation and disaffection in modern life and their impact on rural traditions. His books include *Everyday Life in the Modern World, Introduction to Modernity, The Production of Space,* and *Writings on Cities.*

Robert Bononno is a full-time translator living in New York City. He has taught translation at the Graduate Center of the City University of New York and at New York University. His many translations include *Stanley Kubrick: The Definitive Edition,* by Michel Ciment, and *Cyberculture,* by Pierre Lévy (Minnesota, 2000). He recently received a National Endowment for the Arts grant for the translation of *Isabelle Eberhardt: Seven Years in the Life of a Woman—Letters and Journals.*

Neil Smith was trained as a geographer, and his research explores the broad intersection between space, nature, social theory, and history. He teaches anthropology and geography at the Graduate Center of the City University of New York, where he directs the Center for Place, Culture, and Politics. His books include *The New Urban Frontier* and *Uneven Development: Nature, Capital, and the Production of Space.*